When God Has Put You On Hold

To Dan Anderson —
mentor in the meantime —
Bill Austin
2001

WHEN GOD HAS PUT YOU ON HOLD

BILL AUSTIN

Tyndale House Publishers, Inc.
Wheaton, Illinois

Scripture references, unless otherwise noted, are
from the King James Version of the Bible. Other
quotations are from *The Holy Bible, New
International Version* (NIV), Copyright © 1978 by
New York International Bible Society.

Third printing, January 1988

Library of Congress Catalog Card Number 86-50202
ISBN 0-8423-7989-4
Copyright © 1986 by Bill R. Austin
All rights reserved
Printed in the United States of America

CONTENTS

INTRODUCTION

Waiting for something to happen can be the hardest thing we ever do. Most of us can handle events, decisions—even conflicts better than waiting. That waiting period between events or decisions often creates an "interim anxiety" that can be destructive or paralyzing. Learning to live creatively and productively in the meantime situation should be required training in the human family, and this book is one effort to help.

Such a book seems to be needed. Many wise counselors have told us how to work, how to play, how to worship, how to serve, how to relate, how to improve, and how to negotiate. But very few have anything to say about how to survive in that long interim period when we don't even know what is coming next.

How can we make such an interim time a creative time? How can we turn the waiting line into a production line? How does the night create its own light? Where do we find strength and purpose in a sea of weakness and meaninglessness? What do we do with our hands and minds when there is no work employing them? How do we relate to others who see but can't share our pain? How do we keep futility and despair from conquering our spirits? Most important of all, what kind of a position do we take with God, who seems to have forgotten us? These are the questions we will be confronting in these pages.

The inspiration and idea for this book came from a

sermon by Carlyle Marney, printed in *Pastoral Preaching* (The Bethany Press, St. Louis, Missouri, 1963). At the time, he was pastor of the Myers Park Baptist Church in Charlotte, North Carolina. Prior to that, he had pastored the First Baptist Church of Austin, Texas. But Marney's involvement and influence went far beyond the Baptist pulpit. He was at home in many denominations and countries. He taught and spoke in colleges and seminaries throughout America. In his later years, he operated The Interpreter's House, a place of personal growth and development for fellow ministers.

Carlyle Marney was a superlative preacher, a dedicated churchman, and a prolific writer. But he was also a warm human being. When we had him for a week's preaching in one of our pastorates, I was prepared for the intellectual and theological feast we received, but I was unprepared for his natural and compassionate concern for hurting people.

This side of Marney was revealed eloquently in his sermon "In the Meantime." The message was based on the Old Testament account of the Babylonian Exile, when Israel was overthrown by Babylon and many Israelites were carried away as captives to Babylon. The Babylonian Exile lasted for some seventy years, and the Israelites were constantly trying to adjust and live with the interim anxiety of their meantime. Psalm 137 was written during the Babylonian Exile and expresses the frustration that many of us feel during a long meantime:

> By the rivers of Babylon, there we sat down, yea, we wept, when we remembered Zion. We hanged our harps upon the willows in the midst thereof. For there they that carried us away captive required of us a song; and they that wasted us required of us mirth,

saying, Sing us one of the songs of Zion. How shall we sing the Lord's song in a strange land?

Dr. Marney's message and the theme of this book are based on the advice Jeremiah wrote to these disconsolate Jews in Jeremiah chapter 29.

Marney began his message in vivid and descriptive imagery:

> Most of life is lived *in the meantime*. If a man does not learn to live in the meantime, he is less than half alive. All ages are restless ages to the people who live in them. All times are critical to people who have problems. All roads are weary roads when we have too far to walk. People do not like to wait. This is a badge of our immaturity.
>
> People have always had to live waiting for something. Usually, they wait for peace. They wait for sons to come home from World War III, or brothers to return from World War II, or fathers to get out of World War I. Grandmothers waited for grandfathers to come home from Cuba and the Spanish War. Great-grandmothers waited for the release of the prisoners from Rock Island and Richmond and Memphis. Great-great-great grandmothers waited for the Revolution to grind to an agonizingly slow end. People have always had to live waiting for something: usually peace, or daylight, or recovery of sanity, or husbands to come home, or sons to get well.
>
> People stand in line most of their lives. They wait for a pass, or they wait for a friend, or a break, or payday, or death. They wait for quitting time, or the installments to be paid out, or the doctor to come. They wait for prosperity, or independence, or comfort, or restoration. They wait for their youth to come back, or for power, or for revival. They wait for the Republicans to get in or out, for stocks to go up or down, for the mailman; or sometimes, when they are pastors, they lean back against the corridor wall of the hospital with a fellow and wait for the undertaker

to come. Practically all of life is lived "in the meantime"—some meantime or some other meantime. If a man does not learn to live in the meantime, he finds himself less than half alive.

How can he live when his heart is somewhere else? How can he make it when his dreams have no prospect of coming true? How can he work when his hope is so distant from its consummation? How can he grow in this captivity? How can he endure the silence when he longs for strident sounds and the singing voices? How can he see in this darkness when his eyes were made for light? How can he live in the meantime?[1]

Marney in his sermon described how Jeremiah discovered the answer to the question of living "in the meantime," and passed the answer on to the Israelite exiles in Babylon. He concluded his sermon with this observation:

The paradox of the history of Israel opens here. In all captivities God is at work—*doing* (historizing) his word. All the promises to Israel flower here: The Lord invades, intrudes, breaks through to man's infirmities, *in* man's meantimes—and then? "Then you will call upon me and come and pray to me, and I will hear you. You will seek me and find me; when you seek me with all your heart."[2]

I have used the basic idea of Marney's sermon several times in my own preaching. Every time, without a single exception, the response and interest have been so strong that I am convinced that the feeling of living in the meantime is a universal, almost constant, experience for most people most of the time. Nearly everyone seems to feel that he or she is "on hold," waiting for something to happen.

My own personal pilgrimage has given me a deep

sense of identity with "the waiting ones." It seems I have spent half my life waiting for something. I know the drawn-out agony of sitting by the telephone, pacing the floor, thumbing through magazines, jerking my head up at the sound of an opening door, or whirling around at the sound of long-awaited footsteps. I know the sense of helplessness when you want to do something and all you can do is wait.

I know the taste of bitterness of sitting on the sidelines and others passing me by. I know the gnawing panic of wasted time and passing years that can never be recalled. I know the depression that seeps in because of having to repress anger at being put on hold. I know the foreboding, chest-tightening pain of quiet desperation when realizing that things may never get better. I know also the dread fear that morning light may reveal unwanted answers and burdens too heavy to bear.

Jeremiah wrote his formula for meantime living not only from divine inspiration, but from a lifetime of personal experience in waiting. Likewise, the thoughts of this book are not only from the gleanings of literature but from the countless days and nights of my own waiting and watching and hoping and praying.

Marney was perceptive enough to find Jeremiah answering most of the questions asked in the meantimes of life. I realized that he was really on to something.

I want you to camp with me and the Babylonian exiles beside the river with our harps hanging upon the willow trees. Share with me the moanings of the displaced chosen ones, who cannot sing the Lord's song in a strange land. Let us also look over their shoulders and read Jeremiah's letter again and again. He has, indeed, received a word from the Lord, a word which tells the Israelites, and you and me, how to live in the meantime!

1

Accepting the Reality of Things

Now these are the words of the letter that Jeremiah the prophet sent from Jerusalem unto the residue of the elders which were carried away captives, and to the priests, and to the prophets, and to all the people whom Nebuchadnezzar had carried away captive from Jerusalem to Babylon (Jeremiah 29:1).

"I keep thinking that this is just a bad dream, and I'm going to wake up and things will be right again." How many times have you said that? How many times have counselors, psychologists, and psychiatrists heard distraught clients voice this yearning for things to be different? It is one of the strongest emotions during a meantime situation.

The "meantime" is what we are calling an interim period while we are waiting for things to get better or to work out. If we really enjoyed what we are going through, or if we really felt it was purposeful and productive, we would not be thinking of it as an interim time. So, by its very nature, the meantime attitude has a hard time accepting the present circumstances.

Many meantimes occur because something went wrong and there is a necessary waiting period while things get synchronized and back in working order. Someone has lost his job. A loved one has died. A child has run away from home. A neighbor has been caught in an immoral or unethical act. Family harmony has disintegrated. Investments have failed and our finances are fading. A family member has a terminal illness. The life or safety of a loved one is hanging by a fragile thread.

We can multiply these examples by the varied experiences of our own lives. All of them cause us to cry out for the nightmare to be over, for things to be like they should be. We want sanity, security, and harmony in our world.

Ivan Turgenev once said, "Whatever a man prays for, he prays for a miracle. Every prayer reduces itself to this: Great God, grant that twice two be not four." In my book *How to Get What You Pray For* I take issue with Turgenev and contend that mature prayer consists of asking God how we can work with him to insure that the right two and two get together to produce the perfect four.

I reject Turgenev's generalization that all prayer is a request for God to change the laws of nature. I point out that "there are many sincere Christians who pray daily to know how to serve God better within the natural laws of this created world of his. They do not ask God to change his created order; they ask for the best of all possibilities within that order. They do not pray for evil to vanish from the earth; they pray for right to prevail. They do not pray to be forever free from suffering; they pray for strength to endure."[1]

Although I still reject Turgenev's generalization, I am the first to admit that an intolerable meantime nightmare causes almost everyone to cry out, "Oh, God, please don't let this be true! This can't be happening to me and my family! Please put it back like it used to be." These are the immediate natural responses when things go wrong. It is understandable for us to feel that way at the outset, but continuing to reject reality can be unhealthy and counterproductive.

One of the most common devices of survival during extreme stress is rejection of reality or denial of facts. We somehow believe that if we deny something strongly enough our willpower can change reality.

In the biblical narrative that furnishes the background material for this book, the Israelites could not accept the reality of their exile. They were so stunned by their defeat and captivity that they sat and stared into space or mechanically went through the motions of existence. In Dr. Marney's vivid description, they were:

> . . . huddled in Babylon in camps of canals and artificial rivers, nine hundred miles and a thousand days from the noises and agonies of Jerusalem's fall. Their memories of their dying still scream in their ears; their brains reel and are made stupid by the brazen sounds of pagan worship. Their spirits are overwhelmed by the colossal might of Babylon's military which had smashed them, on horseback, fighting in ranks, riding wheeled instruments of war. They are still befuddled by the clanging chaos of Jerusalem's fall; bogged down now in foreign mud; desolate of any hope for a relieving column to rescue them; promised relief by prophets they knew to be rumor mongers; false hope slipping off into false despair day after day.
>
> Their captors call "Sing us a song!" But how can they sing the songs of the Lord in a strange land? How can they keep the cunning of their skills for revolt alive? How can they forget the debacle that marked the fall of the city? How can they forget their babies crushed in the press at the gate of the city? And how can they hope when no one can set a limit to their hurting? How can they live, in the meantime?[2]

Jeremiah received a special message from the Lord instructing the people how to live in the meantime. He wrote it down in a letter and smuggled it into Babylon where it was passed from hand to hand, elder to elder, camp to camp. It became one of Israel's greatest documents and is preserved for us in Jeremiah chapter 29.

The chapter begins with a clear statement of historical facts: "Now these are the words of the letter that Jeremiah the prophet sent from Jerusalem unto the residue of the elders which were carried away captives, and to the priests, and to the prophets, and to all the people whom Nebuchadnezzar had carried away captive from Jerusalem to Babylon" (Jeremiah 29:1). Then follow the names of some prominent captives and captors. The prophet made the event seem real and final.

Jeremiah was a realist. During most of his ministry he was rejected by his own people because of his practical preaching about Israel's predicament in the political upheavals of the day. He repeatedly foretold the ascendance of Babylon as a world power and insisted that Israel should accept its inevitable destiny and work out a compromise with Babylon. For this he was branded a traitor, imprisoned, and tortured.

Jeremiah was right, of course, and, after a long siege, Jerusalem finally fell to Babylon. The elders, political statesmen, artisans, and business leaders were carried away into Babylon. The first deportation was in 597 B.C. and the second in 587 B.C. This latter date marks the end of Israel as a nation, a status it never recovered until A.D. 1948 when the United Nations set up the state of Israel. So this was a critical event in world history, a political and military victory of Babylon over Israel. It was a definite fact, and Jeremiah knew the people had to accept it before they could learn to live in their meantime exile.

Accepting the reality of their situation was especially hard for Israel because of their sense of destiny and specialness. How could this possibly happen to the chosen people? Likewise, most of us have the same difficulty in accepting the reality of death. Life brings with it a sense of destiny and specialness. I simply cannot imagine not living. Even though I intellectually know I will die some day, I cannot emotionally imagine such a thing. This is similar to the denial of an unimaginable meantime situation.

In her classic work *On Death and Dying,* Dr. Elisabeth Kübler-Ross delineated five distinct emotional stages through which a dying patient passes: denial, anger, bargaining, depression, and acceptance. I have found that all of these stages are also experienced in a serious meantime existence. A long period of waiting without any sign of hope can produce a very real grief process not unlike the grief process of death itself.

This should not surprise us. If a dream has died, or a family has dissolved, a business failed, an opportunity eluded us, or a friend disappointed us, we have felt the sting of death at least upon those areas of our lives. Shakespeare said that "cowards die many times before their death," but so do all ordinary human beings. Loss after loss prepares us for the great final loss. So we should not be surprised to find ourselves reacting in a prolonged interim the same way people do who have learned they are going to die.

The first such reaction, according to Dr. Kübler-Ross, is denial. She said that the almost unanimous reaction is "No, not me, it cannot be true." She described a very typical reaction:

> One of our patients described a long and expensive ritual, as she called it, to support her denial. She was convinced that the X rays were "mixed up"; she asked for reassurance that her pathology report could not possibly be back so soon and that another patient's report must have been marked with her name. When none of this could be confirmed, she quickly asked to leave the hospital, looking for another physician in the vain hope "to get a better explanation for my

troubles." This patient went "shopping around" for many doctors, some of whom gave her reassuring answers, others of whom confirmed the previous suspicion. Whether confirmed or not, she reacted in the same manner; she asked for examination and reexamination, partially knowing that the original diagnosis was correct, but also seeking further evaluations in the hope that the first conclusion was indeed an error, at the same time keeping in contact with a physician in order to have help available "at all times" as she said.[3]

Many of our long waiting spells seem like nightmares. Our life's plan has been thwarted, our routine has been interrupted, our peace has been shattered. We look everywhere for signs of normalcy. We try to get friends and family to reassure us. We turn to employers, bankers, and doctors to give us relief or hope. We keep "shopping around" for someone who will tell us that everything will be right again tomorrow morning.

Dr. Kübler-Ross also emphasized that denial is not merely an initial reaction that is replaced permanently by the next stage of the grief process:

Denial, at least partial denial, is used by almost all patients, not only during the first stages of illness or following confrontation, but also later on from time to time. Who was it who said, "We cannot look at the sun all the time; we cannot face death all the time"? These patients can consider the possibility of their own death for a while but then have to put this consideration away in order to pursue life.[4]

I have experienced this repeatedly in my own meantimes. When I was diagnosed as having multiple sclerosis, I reacted with strong denial, spending time, money, and travel to get a more acceptable diagnosis. Eventually, I learned to accept it and to make alternate plans for

my changed future, but still I would have overpowering
episodes of denial that would almost scream out my
refusal to accept it.

Then we learned that I did not have MS. Instead, I
had five herniated discs which were corrected by surgery. Even then, after release from the dread diagnosis, I
had spells of bitterness and denial that such a thing had
happened to me. To this day, some eight years later, I still
find it hard to believe that my whole life was so drastically changed and that things will never be the same.
While waiting for my life to get back on track, I keep
denying that I have been derailed.

By comparing the meantime experience with the grief
process of death, we can better understand why we feel
some of the things we do and why we react in denial,
anger, and depression. These are normal reactions, and
we should not be ashamed of them. But neither should
we be destroyed by them. Every human emotion has its
opposite counterpart, such as joy and sorrow. The opposite of denial is acceptance, and sooner or later denial
must give way to acceptance if we are to develop and
mature.

Dr. Kübler-Ross insisted that denial can be a healthy
buffer after unexpected shocking news. She said that the
need for denial exists in every patient at times, that day-
dreams about happier things are sometimes essential.
However, there comes a time when the patient gradually
drops his denial and uses less radical defense mecha-
nisms. If the patient has had enough time and has been
given some help in working through the previous stages,
he will reach the stage of acceptance, where he is neither depressed nor angry about his fate.

To accept one's circumstances means in a great part to
accept oneself. When I really accept who and what I am, I

have to accept the limitations along with the potentialities, and the failures as well as the successes. Sören Kierkegaard, the Danish theologian-philosopher, pointed out that the most common despair is that of not choosing, or willing, to be oneself.

In his book *On Becoming a Person,* Carl Rogers described "pure culture" as that moment when the person *is* his fear, *is* his anger, or, *is* his tenderness. The individual becomes more aware of reality as it exists, instead of perceiving it in preconceived categories. Rogers discussed seven stages in the process of becoming a person. The last stage is the acceptance of ownership of feelings and basic trust in one's own process.[5]

The mature stage for which we must strive is the acceptance of ourselves in our meantime. It is not enough to accept facts of history and biology. We must accept ourselves as a part of process. We do not need to be afraid nor ashamed of ourselves during this interim. We are not supermen nor angelic beings; we are flesh-and-blood humans who make mistakes and get hurt. We are vulnerable in a world that is not always friendly, and we are sensitive in a world that is often insensitive.

A common meantime experience is unemployment, a period when men often lose their self-esteem. They are humiliated and feel ashamed that they are not providing for their families. They need a strong dose of reality and hard facts. In many cases it is a matter of national economics or industrial shutdowns, and does not reflect at all on the individual's worth. It is a time when acceptance of one's personal process is absolutely essential. Emotions must not be allowed to obscure facts.

When Harriet, for example, began to have muscle spasms in her face, she casually dismissed it as an emotional "tic." The problem persisted, however, and eventually drove her to doctors, psychiatrists, neurologists, and innumerable tests. She quit her job as a public schoolteacher and went into deep depression. She prayed for healing, for relief, for any kind of help. The help came in the form of an attitude of acceptance.

When Harriet finally began to accept her condition she began to spend more time with her children and to enrich her family life. She found new friends who accepted and encouraged her. She developed a deeper understanding of others who seem to suffer needlessly. She returned to teaching and active church work. Harriet told me, "Life could have been over for me, if I had not come to the point of acceptance."

Thus far, we have talked about the reality of circumstances and the reality of self. But, this does not mean that these are two realities which are mutually exclusive. I am a part of my circumstances and circumstances have become a part of me.

Andras Angyal, in *Foundations for a Science of Personality,* says:

> There is no biological process which is determined entirely organismically or entirely environmentally; it is always a resultant of both factors. There is no environment without an organism. The external world can be called environment only when and in so far as it is in interaction with the organism. Every process which results from the interplay of the organism and its environment is a part of the life process, irrespective of whether it takes place within the body or outside of it.[6]

So, when we speak of accepting the reality of things, we are talking about three areas of reality: the circumstances, the persons involved, and the interaction between persons and circumstances. It might be a helpful exercise for each of us to make a reality list under each of these areas, such as:

The reality of circumstances and events

1. Something really has happened; it is not just my imagination.

2. The clock cannot be turned back; what has been done cannot be undone.

3. This is not all that is happening in the world; other circumstances are at work this very moment.

4. Circumstances have cause and effect; events do not just happen and then go away.

5. No situation is permanent; although it is real, nothing lasts forever.

The reality of self and others

1. I am a vital part of the world; I must not minimize my place and importance.

2. I have eternal worth; nothing that happens to me can diminish that.

3. I am as human as the next person; I am neither perfect nor evil.

4. I am vulnerable; I can and will be hurt if I live long enough.

5. I can survive; what happens *in* me is more important than what happens *to* me.

The reality between people and events

1. I am inseparably linked to my environment and circumstances; I cannot run away.

2. People cause events and events affect people; I can make a difference.

3. Accepting responsibility can be healthy; positive resolutions and change emerge.

4. Wallowing in self-guilt or blaming others gets my perspective out of focus; the task at hand needs to be confronted.

5. Denying that the situation exists is an exercise in futility; I can change only what I admit is real.

In our biblical narrative, Jeremiah appealed to Israel to accept all three of these realities. Rufus Jones, the great Quaker leader, wrote:

> Jeremiah usually took a dark view of things. He did not expect the leopard to change his spots, or the Ethiopian to go white. He looked for no miraculous panacea, no balm in Gilead, to change the hard conditions. But watching a potter remake a spoiled vessel on his potter's wheel, he suddenly had a vision of reality and in a flash he saw that that is what God does with His world. He does not scrap the marred clay. He remakes what has gone wrong. . . . But always the emergence comes through some human individual or some prepared group. It does not come as lightning out of the sky.[7]

In *Man's Search for Meaning,* Viktor E. Frankl introduced his theory of logotherapy (the psychology of meaning) with a brief account of his experiences in Nazi concentration camps. He says that the typical prisoner's initial reaction to imprisonment was one of shock. Among the many shocks was the realization that everything would be taken away. When Frankl tried to protect and preserve his manuscript of a scientific book which contained his life's work, he was ridiculed and rejected with vulgarity and scorn. He says, "At that moment I saw the plain truth and did what marked the culminating point of the first phase of my psychological reaction: I struck out my whole former life."[8]

Very few of us will ever need to strike out drastically our whole former life in order to survive physically. But we may need to accept realistically the fact that the past is over before we can survive emotionally.

Frankl said that another shock was the absolute nakedness with which they were left. "While we were waiting for the shower, our nakedness was brought home to us: we really had nothing except our bare bodies—even minus hair; all we possessed, literally, was our naked existence."[9] Again, few of us will ever be that destitute, but in our interim anxiety we should inventory the reality of our situation. How much do we actually have left? Could we start over again with what we have? Has the most important thing been taken away? Can we survive with what we have if we have to?

In his book Frankl discussed another kind of reality which few of us discover in our unpleasant meantimes, the reality of opportunity and challenge in the meantime itself. He used the term "reality" to emphasize that this is not just an exercise in mental conditioning. He said, "Most men in a concentration camp believed that the real opportunities of life had passed. Yet, *in reality* there was an opportunity and a challenge. One could make a victory of those experiences, turning life into an inner triumph, or one could ignore the challenge and simply vegetate as did the majority of the prisoners!"[10]

You can readily see how this same principle applies to meantime situations. The tragedy of most meantimes is that we do not see them as real life; they are just gaps or voids to be endured until we can get back to our real life. But *in reality,* this meantime may furnish us our greatest opportunity for service or influence.

Also, we need to be realistic in our anxiety over what may happen. We have a natural tendency to expect the worst when in reality the worst may have already happened, and we did survive. The words of Bismarck are especially appropriate here: "Life is like being at the dentist. You always think that the worst is still to come, and yet it is over already."

To this can be added the realistic, and encouraging, words of Nietzsche: "That which does not kill me, makes me stronger."

We are still alive. We have survived. Now, we must review our strengths and weaknesses in comparison with what they were. We should be very realistic. Has our trial made us stronger? It still can if we will determine to be *better* instead of *bitter.*

Viktor Frankl wrote about everything being taken away when they entered the concentration camp. He went on to say that there were some things their captors could not take from them. "What you have experienced, no power on earth can take from you," he said. "Not only our experiences, but all we have done, whatever great thoughts we may have had, and all we have suffered, all this is not lost, though it is past; we have brought it into being. Having been is also a kind of being, and perhaps the surest kind."[11] What marvelous words of encouragement to those of us who feel we have lost everything!

Frankl's explanation was encouraging—that a man's concern, even his despair, over the worthwhileness of life is a *spiritual distress* but by no means a *mental disease.* Again, realism is the key. If we are prone to wonder if we are mentally ill because we are despondent or depressed, we must be realistic about our situation. If things are really as bad as we think (again accepting reality), it is only normal for us to have spiritual distress. In discussing the erratic behavior of the concentration camp inmates, Frankl reminded us that "an abnormal reaction to an abnormal situation is normal behavior."[12] Lessing, the eighteenth-century dramatist, once said, "There are things which must cause you to lose your reason or you have none to lose."

A friend was telling of her mother's calm reaction to the news of her own mother's death and the news that her son had had a heart attack. Everyone else was in distress and grief, but the mother carried on as though nothing had happened. The reason for her unusual behavior was the fact that she has Alzheimer's disease, which slowly but permanently destroys the memory cells of the brain. Her "normal" behavior at tragic news was abnormal. Those who were distressed and frantic were the normal ones because their memories and emotions were still intact.

Experiencing distress and depression may be very realistic and normal in your present situation. Even Jesus Christ is pictured as being often distressed in his spirit. "He sighed deeply in his spirit" (Mark 8:12). "He groaned in the spirit and was troubled" (John 11:33). "Now is my soul troubled and what shall I say?" (John 12:27). "He was troubled in spirit" (John 13:21). He was even called the man of sorrows.

This fact is not an excuse for self-pity or a license for being disagreeable. It is simply a reminder that normal people do react with a negative spirit to negative events. It is realistic for us to be hurt, despondent, even angry if circumstances warrant it. However, it becomes unrealistic and unhealthy for us to stay in that state. We must move on through the next stages of healing and recovery.

The final reality which Frankl said is essential in survival is the reality of choice. This may be the hardest for us to accept if we feel that we have been the innocent victims of cruel circumstances. Did we have a choice? Frankl's reply would be that we always have a choice as to how the circumstances will affect us. He rejected the theory that man is no more than a product of many conditional and environmental factors:

> Man is *not* fully conditioned and determined; he determines himself whether to give in to conditions or stand up to them. In other words, man is ultimately self-determining. Man does not simply exist, but always decides what his existence will be, what he will become in the next moment.[13]

Frankl used his personal observations in the concentration camp to illustrate the reality of choice.

> The experiences of camp life show that man does have a choice of action. There were enough examples, often of a heroic nature, which proved that apathy can be overcome, irritability suppressed. Man *can* preserve a vestige of spiritual freedom, of independence of mind, even in such terrible conditions of psychic and physical stress.
>
> We who lived in concentration camps can remember the men who walked through the huts comforting others, giving away their last piece of bread. They may have been few in number, but they offer sufficient proof that everything can be taken from a man but one thing: the last of the human freedoms—to choose one's attitude in any given set of circumstances, to choose one's own way.[14]

Jeremiah's message to the Israelites in Babylon was a call for accepting reality. He cited names, places, and dates to drive home the reality of their defeat and captivity. He never played games or colored facts. In a straightforward manner he said, "Israel has been crushed and Jerusalem destroyed. You have been carried away captive. You are forced to live in a foreign land. You are not free to come home. These are facts and realities. But it is also a fact that you are still alive, and you can make of your exile what you will. There is work to be done. There are relationships to be nurtured. There are roots to put down. There is a future to prepare for. You have the choice of deciding how you will handle all of this. The past is a reality which cannot be changed. The present is a reality placed in your hands. The future is a reality waiting to be shaped by you!"

2

Seeing God Behind the Scenes

Thus saith the Lord of hosts, the God of Israel, unto all that are carried away captives, whom I have caused to be carried away from Jerusalem unto Babylon. . . . For I know the thoughts that I think toward you, saith the Lord, thoughts of peace, and not of evil, to give you an expected end (Jeremiah 29:4, 11).

Where is God? You have believed in him and served him and now you really need him. But the nights are dark and the days are long and your prayers are unanswered. There seems to be no evidence that God is working in your behalf. In fact, events seem to be mocking your faith and stretching your patience to the snapping point.

Where is God? There is perhaps no question that is asked more often or more urgently by those who wait. In every age, in countless circumstances, and in all languages the plaintive cry has been flung heavenward—Where is God?

If there is a God, why doesn't he do something? Why doesn't he straighten out this mess and bring this long night of waiting to an end? This is probably the most unoriginal question we can ask, for since the beginning of time men have been asking it. But that doesn't keep us from adding our voice to the cry, and it is normal for us to do so. In fact, asking, "Where is God?" at least shows that we have taken the biblical message seriously.

The God of the Bible is (1) a God who is good, (2) a God who is all powerful, (3) a God who reveals himself, and (4) a God who communicates with man.

When one or more of these traits of God seem to be missing, it is only natural for the believer to be jarred or thrown off balance. If evil is prevailing, where is the God who is good and powerful? If there is no evidence of divine presence, where is the God who reveals himself? If there is no clear message from the Lord, where is the God who communicates?

If these questions keep invading our meantime, it is not necessarily a lack of faith. It may mean that we have taken our religion so seriously that we expected God to do something by now and we simply don't understand why he hasn't.

We may never understand, and we may never be satisfied with encouraging words from well-meaning friends, but we can develop a distinctive posture of faith to see us through this long interim of hurting and waiting. This posture of faith does not demand immediate divine intervention, but accepts constant divine participation that is always working behind the scenes.

In the scriptural account that forms the basis for this book, the children of Israel were in exile in Babylon, crying out in brokenhearted agony, "Where is God?" From the looks of things, God had done nothing to stop the destruction of Jerusalem by the barbaric Babylonians. He had stood silently by while the finest and fittest of Israel's people were carried away captive, and he seemed to be aloof and uninvolved during their long captivity.

But, in the first words of Jeremiah's letter to the exiles, God said that he was the one who caused them to be carried away from Jersualem unto Babylon (v. 4). Later on in the letter, God made it clear that his plan and purpose was for Israel's eventual benefit and good end (v. 11). These two verses give the foundation for a strong posture of faith. Verse 4 reveals that God is working even when we cannot see him, and verse 11 insists that God has our welfare in his heart and plan.

Through Jeremiah's pen, God wrote a strong and clear message that he had not been silent or weak or inactive in all of Israel's sufferings. Even in their darkest tragedy, God was working behind the scenes to preserve a faithful remnant, to allow capable leaders to be taken to Babylon where they would learn new ways for the future Israel, and to plan for restoration and redemption.

Naturally, Israel could see only the defeat and the despair. They could not see God at work behind the scenes. Neither can you and I. That is why it must be a posture of faith. "Now faith is the substance of things hoped for, the evidence of things not seen" (Hebrews 11:1).

I know how hard it is to keep believing when there seems to be no hope. I know that unanswered prayer can turn one's meantime into doubt and bitterness. But I also know that a resolute posture of faith can restore hope, conquer doubt, and erase bitterness. In using the term "posture of faith," I am not talking about the kind of faith that takes control and changes things the way we want them (the power of faith). I believe there are times when a faith such as that needs to be exercised. But most of our meantime interims need a faith that believes God is working behind the scenes even if we can't see the evidence (the posture of faith).

Knowing the difference between the *power* of faith and the *posture* of faith may keep us from losing faith altogether. We must not be distraught when people tell us that our faith is weak because we haven't been able to change circumstances by our prayers. We must remember that the strongest faith may be the quiet posture of believing that God hasn't forsaken us when all the facts indicate that he has.

Shadrach, Meshach, and Abednego were taunted by Nebuchadnezzar about their God when they were about to be cast into the fiery furnace. They said to the king: "O Nebuchadnezzar, we do not need to defend ourselves before you in this matter. If we are to be thrown into the blazing furnace, the God we serve is able to save us from it, and he will rescue us from your hand, O king. But even if he does not, be it known to you, O king, that we will not serve your gods" (Daniel 3:16-18, NIV).

Notice their progressive posture of faith: (1) our God is able to deliver us; (2) we believe he is going to deliver us; (3) but if he does not, we will die serving and worshiping him anyway.

If may sound like weak faith to put in the "if he does not," but to me it is the real proof of genuine faith. The big question that every honest person tries to answer is, What will I do if he doesn't?[1]

How can we develop this posture of faith that sees God behind the scenes? Three questions need to be considered and resolved before we can have the peace such a posture can give us.

Is Faith a Cop-out?

When we can't seem to make a difference or change a situation or hasten a conclusion, are we taking the easy way out by saying that we believe in God anyway?

No, faith is not a cop-out, nor is it an easy approach to problems. It is a lot easier not to believe sometimes than it is to believe.

Without a posture of faith that believes God is at work, we would soon lose our hopes and perhaps our minds. In *The Sinner of Saint Ambrose,* Robert Raynolds wrote, "A sense of God is the root of spiritual sanity."

Everyone needs something or someone to help him make it through the night. Rather than turning to destructive aids such as drugs and alcohol, we can discover the constructive aids which God provides through friends, family, counselors, fellow Christians, prayer, good literature, and his personal presence.

We cannot develop a strong posture of faith if we feel foolish or weak or ashamed to admit the need for assurance that God is still with us. In *Street of Knives,* Cyril Harris described the following scene which underscores the universal need for faith.

> Blennerhassett heard behind him the sound of someone setting foot on the little bridge and coming towards him, but he did not look up to see who it was. "Have you lost something overboard, Squire?" Hugh asked him, because Blennerhassett was staring into the water at the side of the bridge.
> "Aye, Hugh. That I have. . . . Do you see this handrail?" Blennerhassett said. "I'm leaning on it, and you are. That's what it's here for. To lean on. To keep you and me from falling in. Well, that's what I've lost. Handrail. Something to hold me back when I get too near the edge. It has to be strong, and it has to be there. Men call it God. I'm looking for it."

Denice M. was fifteen months old when her mother's best friend accidentally backed her car over the little girl's head. Denice received a severe concussion which sent one of her eyes reeling to the side. She had vast skull fractures, and remained in a coma for several days. During those long meantime hours of waiting to see if their daughter would live and be normal again, her parents rediscovered that faith is more than a cop-out for weak souls.

Her mother told me about those anxious days of waiting: "Knowing that we would need our strength to care for her, we accepted a friend's invitation to rest and sleep in their home near the hospital. On the bedside table lay our host's Bible. Needing so much to feel God's assurance that our Denice would be all right, we picked up the Bible which fell open to John 9:1-7, the account of Jesus healing a blind man. The following night the Bible opened again to John 11:1-45, the account of Jesus raising Lazarus to life. We felt strengthened and encouraged to believe that God could perform a miracle for us too."

After seven days in intensive care and seven more in another room, little Denice came out of her coma. Although she had to learn to walk and talk all over again, she eventually recovered completely.

Her mother says with clear confidence, "God's Word, the Bible, and the messages recorded there, the various applications of each thought written there, the privilege of prayer and the companionship of God—these are the tools for getting through ordeals."

Once you have satisfied yourself that faith is not a superficial escape, but a practical necessity for meaningful existence, you need to ask the next question about the apparent absence of God in your situation.

Does Silence Mean Absence?

The God of the Bible reveals himself and communicates with man. When revelation and communication seem to be shut off it seems natural to ask, Where is God?

Most believers have a hard time understanding Aldous Huxley in *Brave New World* when he has the World Controller say, "God manifests himself in different ways to different men. In pre-modern times he manifested himself as the being that's described in these books. Now . . ."

"How does he manifest himself now?" asked the Savage.

"Well, he manifests himself as an absence; as though he weren't there at all."

Faith responds that silence does not necessarily mean absence. What may appear to be the triumph of evil may instead be the patient, deliberate hand of God working out the providential details of his plan.

When Joseph's brothers saw him on the seat of power in Egypt they feared his revenge for betraying him when he was younger. The wise and magnanimous Joseph told them not to be afraid: "You intended to harm me, but God intended it for good" (Genesis 50:20, NIV).

Centuries later, Joseph's descendants had a hard time seeing the hand of God in their Babylonian exile. Yet, history has seen an active God, not an absent God in the exile. Paul Scherer wrote,

> God had chosen them for a purpose that wasn't always theirs; and when they made up their minds not to go along with it, he had to set himself against them. He swept them into exile, captives trudging across the burning sands toward Babylon. Against them only because from start to finish he was never anything else but for them.[2]

Scherer was describing the posture of faith I am talking about. Even when it seems that God is against us, we must believe that he has always been, and still is, for us.

We have all quoted many times the encouraging words of Romans 8:31, "If God be for us, who can be against us." But, we may not realize that Paul gave this word of hope within the context of describing the terrible meantime the early Christians were enduring: "tribulation, distress, persecution, famine, nakedness, peril, sword . . . sheep for the slaughter" (Romans 8:35, 36).

In the midst of all that comes the clarion sound of assurance—God is with us, and nothing "shall be able to separate us from the love of God, which is in Christ Jesus our Lord."

Dietrich Bonhoeffer, a brilliant young theologian, was executed by the Nazis in an extermination camp in 1945. Bonhoeffer emphasized the theme "the world come of age," by which he meant that adulthood marks the time of accountability and responsibility. He insisted that righting the wrongs of the world is our responsibility and should not be looked at as a responsibility of heaven.

Whether we agree with all of Bonhoeffer's thoughts or not, his works are well worth our reading. Living in the meantime of World War II and the horror of Nazi concentration camps, he found it imperative to say something about the silence and apparent absence of God in a world being destroyed by evil men.

Bonhoeffer affirmed a God who was weak in the world, but this weakness was the form of his power.

> God is weak and powerless in the world, and that is exactly the way, the only way, in which he can be with us and help us. . . . Man's religiosity makes him look in his distress to the power of God in the world. . . . The Bible, however, directs him to the power-lessness and suffering of God; only a suffering God can help.[3]

Some who read these words will be stimulated to learn more about Bonhoeffer's concept of divine "weakness" and human responsibility. Others will insist that God is not powerless, that he is merely biding his time until the right moment for action.

Both viewpoints, I believe, can coexist in a Christian posture of faith. God expects us to do all that we can, but he has not left us alone. He has given us the instruction of the Scriptures, the example of his Son, and the guidance of the Spirit. He is working even now in the events of our lives and in the lives of others who will influence our destiny. He is preparing us for the time when we will be given the opportunity to choose the best he has for us. Professor Charles Hartshorne says that God chooses the greatest possible good for us and then gives us the freedom to confirm or reject that choice.[4]

Where is God? In *The Waiting Father,* Helmut Thielicke reminded us that God is waiting and watching. He wrote, "The ultimate theme of the Prodigal Son is not the faithlessness of men, but the faithfulness of God."[5] I think Bonhoeffer would feel very comfortable with the Father-God image in the prodigal son story, a Father who waits in love and reserved power to give all that he has to the child who finally comes home. No, silence does not mean absence.

Many times parents must remain silent and let their children work out their problems. But their silence does not mean absence. They are very much present in concern and compassion, and in readiness to help in a critical emergency. When human parents remember how hard it is to be silent when their children are hurting or making mistakes, they should realize how deeply God feels for them although they may not see his hand at work.

The third question naturally follows this second question about the silence of God.

How Does God Work?

If our posture of faith affirms that God is working behind the scenes even when we can't see him, just exactly how is he working?

I suppose the ultimate posture of faith would be to let God be God, that is, let him work as he chooses without ever asking about his methods.

The human mind, however, is always asking how, and even when led by faith, we still want to know more about our God and how he is dealing with our situation.

One of the best ways to understand how God works is to take the negative approach, eliminating unacceptable and unbiblical images of God that have cluttered our thinking. This is the approach J. B. Phillips took in his book, *Your God Is Too Small.* The first half of the book discredited images of "unreal Gods," such as resident policemen, parental hangover, grand old man, meek and mild, God-in-a-box, managing director, etc.[6]

As an exercise, we might try writing down as many descriptions of God as we can call to mind and then back off and look at them. Do these really describe the God of the Bible, the Lord and Father of Jesus Christ?

What has all this to do with our interminable meantime? Everything! Our concept of God and how he works will shape the posture of our faith while we are waiting.

For instance, one of our most common concepts of God is referred to by theologians as *deus ex machina,* the God of the machine. This is a term taken from the theater. *Deus ex machina* is an emergency device used by incompetent playwrights. A poor writer has a way of getting his characters involved in situations that are so complicated and desperate that there is no solution within the context of the situation itself. At such a juncture, the playwright, in a frantic effort to make things come out right, is forced to introduce a *deus ex machina*. In some old plays this took the form of an entrance by a god, angel, or fairy, actually lowered from the stage flies by machinery, hence the term "the god of the machine." The same principle is applied in the modern theater when the playwright brings into the plot a foreign character or action, the sole purpose of which is to rescue a situation that the author cannot control out of the resources of the plot itself.

Too often we think of God as *deus ex machina*. Regardless of how big a mess we get ourselves into, in the back of our minds we believe that God will swoop down on the stage at the last moment and rescue us.

Vernard Eller says that man does not have to resort to a *deus ex machina* because there is a Playwright who has already written a script which avoids the need for such an intervention. Man writes his own script too often and gets himself into hopeless situations, but "as soon as man is willing to accept his script from God the Playwright, he loses all need for a *deus ex machina*."[7]

Eller then moved from the analogy of the stage to one of the jungle, examining the ways one might handle men in such a setting. One might build a stockade to keep the jungle out and the men in. Religion has often been inclined to use God the Stockade for security and protection, "but just as *deux ex machina* was a desperate measure to save an incompetent playwright, so is God the Stockade a desperate measure to save a cowardly explorer."[8]

Eller asks us to consider, instead, God the Beacon. Rather than being on the perimeter as a stockade, God is in the center of the jungle, sending out messages to man the explorer. God is behind man rather than always set before his face. "The explorer knows he can explore only as long as he maintains communication with the center; there are no stockade walls to bump him into remembrance."[9]

These analogies, like all analogies, have their limitations, but it might help us to have a fresh thought about our predicament. Have we been depending on the *deus ex machina* to get us out of our meantime, or have we been expecting God the Stockade to keep the jungle dangers away from us? It will help strengthen both our faith and resolve to have a more mature concept of God than these.

"What finally must a Christian understanding of God preserve?" asks C. W. Christian in *Shaping Your Faith*. Answering his own question, Christian wrote:

> God must be sovereign, that is sufficiently in control to give direction to life and history. And he must be love. If he is not love, he is not God, and human values become lost in a hostile world. If he is not sovereign, his love is sentimental and finally pointless. The Christian God is both sovereign and love. Or better yet, he is "sovereign love."[10]

In answer, then, to the question of how God does work, he works as the Center, the Beacon, communicating with man the explorer. He works as the Playwright who has a script which requires no *deus ex machina*. He works as Sovereign Love in control of his world, but leading and guiding through love, not force.

The question of evil in a world created by a God of sovereign love has always been an intellectual problem for man. Why are we having to go through our trial if God is sovereign and if he is love?

None of us knows the ultimate answer to that universal cry, but I recently came across a beautiful thought which helped me during a particular time when I felt deserted by God. Helmut Thielicke wrote, in *How to Believe Again,*

> Everything must go through him before it hits me. And if it then hits me I at least know that it has passed his inspection and gotten his "OK." Isn't it true that whether something is tough or easy in my life depends ultimately on one thing: whether I can receive it from his hand or not? If I only see a dark, anonymous fate as the sender of everything that hits me, then it all becomes anxious, comfortless, and hopeless. If, however, I see his greetings on my way, then I always receive a positive order, then I know that it is not in vain, that it must serve my best interests, and that it will be creative. Then I know that his higher thoughts have already prepared the goal for me, while I, with my human thoughts, am still groping in the dark.[11]

Thielicke here gives another description of what I call the posture of faith, one that sees God working behind the scenes of our meantime. This does not mean that God is to be blamed for our situation. Many tragic things happen which clearly cannot be the products of a loving heavenly Father. But, in the midst of the tragedy, God is working to bring good out of evil, strength out of weakness, and light out of darkness.

Dorothy lost her son Robert in an automobile accident when he was nineteen. Her world was shattered and her faith severely tested. She went through long agonizing months of depression and anger. She felt deserted by God, friends, and church. Release from her anguish came only after she went before the church and asked their forgiveness for her bitterness. Then she began to put her feelings and thoughts into writing. I asked her to let me share with you some of her deepest insights into her pain and her faith in God's goodness. She never wrote about God taking, only about his giving. Life became the most precious gift of all, and she has become radiantly aware of every facet of that gift. These words were written in the raw pain and struggling faith of her meantime:

> As you grow older you accept the idea that one day you are likely to lose your husband or parents, but not your child. And certainly not at such a young age. This shock remains with me now—my son frozen forever in time as the charming, mischievous, high-spirited young man he was at his death. Even today it is acutely painful and I miss his laughter, temper, and the sheer joy of his companionship.
>
> Instead of dwelling on loss, I try to bring back all the best memories. In doing so, Robert's image lives forever in the forefront of my mind. Only my faith has given me the strength to bear this sorrow and try to balance it against the blessings.
>
> I tell myself that God gave my children many gifts—spirit, beauty, intelligence, the capacity to make friends (Robert had more than his share of this gift), and to inspire respect. There was only one gift that was limited to Robert—length of life. Dear God, I miss him so.
>
> Do I question God? Yes. Do I wonder about his reasons? Yes. I cannot fully understand, I am simply accepting his wisdom. Although I grieve, I go on for I believe acceptance is the meaning and test of faith, and God wants us to take what blessings he has given us. If we yield to grief, if we let our emotional and mental energy be absorbed by our losses, we lose something greater still—life itself, God's greatest gift.

Dorothy was not the first nor the last to have her world shattered by tragedy. We ourselves may be reeling from a terrible blow, but like Dorothy we can survive this nightmare by seeing God as a caring Father who provides the strength we desperately need.

Many people and events that will somehow affect our lives are right now crisscrossing and entertwining. God is at work among them all, and he has not forgotten where we are and what we need. At the right time we will feel his finger on our hearts and hear him whisper, "I am here, child, if you will only believe." We must be ready at any moment to be able to say sincerely, "Lord, I believe."

3

Getting Back to Work

Build ye houses, and dwell in them; and plant gardens, and eat the fruit of them (Jeremiah 29:5).

Our meantime existence may have stripped us of energy and robbed us of purpose. We sit and stare into space. We have to force ourselves to do the least essentials of living. Our spirits have been beaten down and we can't seem to pull ourselves back up. Then we discover an odd fact of life: that spiritual and emotional illness is often cured by strong physical measures. We have to learn, as Israel did, that the best medicine may be common sweat.

The first two steps in learning how to live in the meantime were mental and philosophical—accepting the reality of things, and seeing God behind the scenes. The third step is physical and practical: getting back to work.

A few years ago, I learned the amazing therapeutic value of a daily schedule of ordinary work. In the midst of a busy pastorate, I became suddenly and critically ill with a wide variety of neurological symptoms. Several reputable physicians diagnosed my condition as multiple sclerosis, and I began a series of experimental treatments in one of the nation's leading medical centers.

Rather than improving, I continued to deteriorate and became almost useless as a pastor. I was still able to preach most Sundays by sitting on a stool and greatly restricting my time and participation. I could not make regular pastoral visits and met only spasmodically with staff and committees.

The long days stretched into longer weeks and endless months. The pain, weakness, disability, and depression were almost more than I could cope with. In fact, I doubt that I would have coped had I not forced myself to work in new and creative ways.

I began a vigorous ministry of visitation via the telephone. Every day I had a certain time to call prospects, members who were ill, and church leaders. I used my time in the bed to write, design new programs, and plan the various ministries of our church. I began to have staff meetings and committee meetings in my home, often around my bed. The days went faster and I was able to sleep better at night because I was working regular hours, although in different ways than before.

However, my physical condition continued to worsen until we realized that I was not going to be able to function as the church needed. It seemed only right to release the church from a sick pastor and so we began to make plans for medical retirement.

Then, in a very dramatic way, we discovered that I did not have MS after all. I had five herniated discs which were causing so many different problems and symptoms that it seemed natural to assume I had MS. I spent the summer of 1976 in the hospital with three back surgeries, which successfully corrected my problem.

The road back, however, was much longer and harder than I expected. The many months of pain and weakness had taken their toll. The heavy medication had left numerous adverse effects, and the three surgeries so close together had almost wiped out what remaining strength I had.

The long weeks of recuperation brought more despair and depression. After I knew I did not have an incurable disease, I was eager to get back to work, but it seemed I would never regain the strength I needed.

Remembering the healing value of working when I had thought I had MS, I determined to force myself to recover the same way. I had already completed my course work toward the Ph.D. before I became ill, but I abandoned any hope of writing my doctoral dissertation when I was struck down. Now seemed the right time to get back to work on it, so I made contact with the school officials, who were very cooperative. They sent books to me that I could not get locally, and encouraged me in many ways.

My wife fixed me a lap board that I could use for writing in bed or in a lounge chair. I set a regular schedule for going to work every day and stayed with it religiously. I became engrossed in the work and prospect of actually getting my Ph.D. after all. There was no place or time now for self-pity and depression. I worked long, hard, concentrated hours, day by day. Even after I was able to go back to the church for regular office hours, I managed to continue the dissertation work on my days off. As a result, the following spring I walked across the stage (which I could not have done a year earlier) and received my Ph.D. Perhaps an even more important result was what the enforced work load had done for me psychologically during my long meantime.

I had learned the true value of Charles Kingsley's advice: "Thank God every morning when you get up that you have something to do that day which must be done, whether you like it or not."

The Israelites could not stand to face the dawn of every new day in their Babylonian captivity. They could not sing the songs of Zion in a strange land. They hung their harps on willow trees and sat down by the river to mourn the fall of Jerusalem.

But Jeremiah would not listen to their self-pity. He

jarred them out of their despair with practical, everyday instructions. His first specific instruction was not a philosophical or theological statement; it was a practical call to get to work.

He knew how much they missed Jerusalem, and he knew how much they grieved over their slaughtered loved ones. But he also knew that they had to keep living. They had to have houses and clothes and food. There were families depending on them, children whose very survival was waiting for them to get back to work. Also, their own emotional sanity demanded that they plunge into the everyday chores again as quickly as possible.

In his sermon "In the Meantime," which we acknowledged in the introduction, Dr. Marney said,

> In the meantime of captivity, do the everyday jobs, do the next thing! There is healing in the performance of the prosaic. More than a few times I have turned with some friend from the cot where death has just slacked a jaw, or from the hearth where death has just sent a telegram, to find a watering pot or a broom to use. "Miss Myrtle, your flowers are dry and brittle, you haven't watered them." Or, "Ruby, let's work!" Sometimes the only thing to do is work— anything if its done like an automaton—no thinking— just work. Or sometimes I say, "Let's make the lists now of all we have to call." Or I say, "Let's gather up the things now." The next thing! Sometimes it's all one can do because it's all there is—and Jeremiah says there is a healing in it. Do the next thing!"[1]

At such a time, we probably don't feel like working. Our meantime has sapped us of energy and enthusiasm. We can no longer focus on the vision of our completed destiny because the drudgery of the immediate is consuming our interest. We shouldn't try to recover the vision all at once. Rather than try to get the long look again, we should just take it one day at a time—maybe when the hurt is so bad, just one hour at a time.

Robert Louis Stevenson said, "Anyone can carry his burden, however hard, until night fall. Anyone can do his work, however hard, for one day."

Jeremiah knew that houses are not built in a day and gardens are not planted and reaped in a day. The healing would come in the long, tedious, back-breaking labor day after day until they had sweated all the poison of bitterness and sorrow out of their systems. We shouldn't think about whether we feel like working, or speculate about whether we will even finish the job. We must get to work, immediately and aggressively, tackling the next thing that has to be done.

The temptation to retreat into religion is very strong when we feel that the world has put us on hold. This seems the ideal time to pray, to reflect, to ponder, to "get closer to God." In their proper time, those are spiritual exercises we must engage in. Physical work should be considered as a partner, not an enemy of spiritual growth and inward peace.

Rufus Jones, the great Quaker leader, said:

> We want to secure a life which combines contemplation and action, an inward serenity and a spirit of adventure. . . . The principle of calm is not attained by a method of detachment and withdrawal. The rich and genuine life of calm and adventure comes rather by a new and greater attachment, by the formation of a profounder loyalty and the discovery of a wider reference of interests.[2]

Don't be misled by those who insist that truly spiritual people are not concerned about the physical work and products of this world. I think it is very significant that when God decided to take on human flesh, he did it in the body of a carpenter, not a philosopher.

One day while St. Francis of Assisi was hoeing his garden, some of his young disciples stopped by to engage him in theological speculation. One of them asked him what he would do with the rest of the day if he were to receive a message that this was his last day to live. Francis immediately answered, "First I would finish hoeing my garden."

Most of us would rush to prayer or to the Bible or try to get ourselves into an acceptable spiritual condition. Francis had learned the secret of spiritual peace in doing the task at hand.

I saw an updated version of that story while watching television in 1969. Neil Armstrong had just completed his historical voyage to the moon and was being interviewed on a television talk show. The host asked him numerous questions about his feelings on being the first man on the moon. Then, he posed this question to the famous astronaut: "Neil, what would you have done if, while on the moon, you had received word from control center that your engine was not working properly and that you would not be able to launch and reattach with the command module. Assuming you had only six hours of oxygen left, and stranded on the moon with a malfunctioning engine, how would you have spent those six hours?"

The interviewing host was probably expecting Neil to say something religious or patriotic, but instead, he quickly replied, "I would have spent every minute working on that engine!"

I like that answer and I think our Lord would like it. Jesus himself said, "I must work the works of him that sent me, while it is day: the night cometh, when no man can work" (John 9:4).

This sounds like a New Testament echo of the Old Testament admonition: "Whatever your hand finds to do, do it with all your might, for in the grave, where you are going, there is neither working nor planning nor knowledge nor wisdom" (Ecclesiastes 9:10, NIV).

Those who are tempted to spend the waiting time talking to friends and family, trying to solve things by going over and over them, need to consider the wisdom of Proverbs 14:23: "All hard work brings a profit, but mere talk leads only to poverty" (NIV). Spiritual and emotional poverty are the result of endless talking in lieu of hard work.

"But, if our meantime has been brought about because of the illness or death of a loved one, doesn't it seem disrespectful to go on working as though nothing had happened?" someone may ask.

I am not suggesting that. If something serious, perhaps tragic, has happened, we need to respond to it appropriately and unselfishly, giving as much of ourselves and our time as is needed to those who have been affected by the event. But, we must remember that one of the best tributes we can pay to those who matter to us is to give a higher significance, even a holy stature, to everyday life and its demands.

In *Nostromo,* Joseph Conrad reminded us, "For life to be large and full, it must contain the care of the past and of the future in every passing moment of the present. Our daily work must be done to the glory of the dead, and for the good of those who come after."

Life must go on to have any meaning at all, and we can keep the pulse of love and hope beating by seeing that ordinary chores and ordinary events do not come to a halt. Dostoevski's friends celebrated Christmas in Siberia; the wrecks of men held at Andersonville tried to build houses out of stumps; and the Count of Monte Cristo had a vine and a flower to watch in his cell.

The Israelites learned much during their seventy-year exile, and those years dramatically changed many things about the religion and culture of Israel. Perhaps the greatest thing they learned and the greatest thing they achieved for their posterity was the abiding value of faithfulness to the common task at hand. Building houses and planting gardens shook the people out of their despair and started them on the road to recovery.

In *You Can't Go Home Again,* Thomas Wolfe has George write,

> I learned much, many true and hopeful things. I learned, first of all, that one must work, that one must do what work he can, as well and ably as he can, and that it is only the fool who repines and longs for what is vanished. . . . I learned to accept that essential fact without complaint, but, having accepted it, to try to do what was before me, what I could do, with all my might.

4

Considering the Family

Take ye wives, and beget sons and daughters; and take wives for your sons, and give your daughters to husbands, that they may bear sons and daughters; that ye may be increased there, and not diminished (Jeremiah 29:6).

In verse 5 Jeremiah told Israel to build houses; in verse 6 he told them to build homes. There is a difference, you know. Sinclair Lewis, in *Babbitt,* wrote, "In fact there was but one thing wrong with the Babbitt house: It was not a home."

While grieving over their lost houses in Jerusalem, Israel was in danger of losing their homes in Babylon. They were so burdened and depressed that they could not carry on the ordinary functions of family life. Jeremiah wrote to remind them that they were going to be in Babylon for seventy years, and the only family life any of them would know would be in that foreign city. So, he said, "Revive the old traditions and continue the essential relationships. Let your children and grandchildren know the kind of family life you knew back in Jerusalem. Let them marry and start their own homes. Show them that they can still love and be loved even in an alien environment and an uncertain meantime."

Commenting on this particular verse, Dr. Carlyle Marney wrote:

> In the meantime, there is a fellowship to be considered. The Lord advised the Jews to see to their wives and sons and daughters in this foreign land. None of the meantimes must be allowed to cut across

this fundamental relationship. This is an order of creation: to see to it in the meantime, any meantime. Grief over a lost estate of prosperity must not filter down to soak the children with senseless tears. Loss of domain must not creep into the house of a daughter and suck her under grief, too. Despair at being unable to move or pay or deny or beg or acquire or restore must not throttle down to emptiness the thrust and zeal and power of fellowship. Let no one impose his own meantime on younger hearts and weaker backs. Let him carry his meantime out of sight.

I have seen with my own eyes the violation of this principle from Jeremiah's letter destroy the witness of a virile Christian home, wreck the health of a daughter, alienate a husband, distort two wonderful boys, and put an ailing mother-in-law in an institution in less than two years. There is a fellowship—even of exile—even of suffering—that must not be distorted in the meantime.[1]

Maintaining the essential bonds of relationships during a stressful interim requires deliberate effort and patience.

1. *Symbolic events and actions* should be maintained with persistence and determination. Jeremiah insisted that they carry on the Jewish traditions of marriage, birth, and family. "Marry and have sons and daughters; find wives for your sons and give your daughters in marriage, so that they too may have sons and daughters" (29:6, NIV).

Those routine traditions that we took for granted during normal times take on a special significance during times when we have to consciously work at making them happen. A wedding ceremony has in it a poignant holiness during wartime. The birth of a child, while bringing extra responsibility, also brings new hope during unemployment or illness. The ceremony of baptism can spark the beginning of new resolves and the righting of old wrongs.

The family must continue to worship together regularly. Thanksgiving, Christmas, and Easter must take on greater meaning than ever and receive excited participation. Every birthday must be celebrated enthusiastically and lovingly. Every person must be made to feel that he is loved and valued and that all things the family has stood for still matter deeply.

Little things must not be overlooked. Sometimes our most enduring values are represented by symbols which might seem trifling to outsiders. In *The River,* Rumer Godden reminds us:

> Every family has something, when it has left home, that is for it a symbol of home, that, for it, for ever afterwards, brings home back. It may be a glimpse of the dappled flank of a rocking horse, a certain pattern of curtain, of firelight shining on a brass fender, of light on the rim of a plate; it may be a saying, sweet or sharp . . . it may be a song or a sound; the sound of a lawn mower, or the swish of water, or of birds singing at dawn; it may be a custom (every family has different customs), or a taste: of a special pudding or burnt treacle tart or dripping toast; or it may be a scent or a smell: of flowers, or furniture polish or cooking, toffee or sausages, or saffron bread or onions or boiling jam. These symbols are all that are left of that last world in our new one.

Jeremiah was pleading for the exiles to hold on to their cherished symbols and traditions in their new world. Throughout all of history, the Jewish people have been most tenacious and successful in holding on to traditions, symbols, and customs although, as a people, they have been displaced and scattered throughout the earth time and again. They continue to be a people with strong traditions and families. The two seem to go together. As we try to strengthen the traditions in our meantime, we may notice that the family will probably be strengthened at the same time.

Survival itself often depends on the little things which have become central. Many distraught travelers have held on until the dawn by getting a tight grip on precious memories and significant relationships.

Dr. Viktor Frankl, cited earlier, would ask his patients, "Why do you not commit suicide?" The answers were varied. In one life there was love for one's children to tie to. In another life, there was a talent to be used. In a third, perhaps there were only lingering memories worth preserving. Dr. Frankl then attempted to weave these slender threads of a broken life into a firm pattern of meaning and responsibility.[2] What may seem trivial to others could be the salvation we need for ourselves and our families, so we should hold on to it.

2. *Someone must assume responsibility and take initiative.* Jeremiah's instructions recognized the tendency for people to wait for someone else to lead, but he called for decision and action. He knew that someone had to break out of the pack and lead the way back to normalcy.

Depression has a strange leveling effect. People who once felt favored and blessed suddenly feel that they are just like everyone else, or even worse. "Natural born leaders" often become passive and reclusive when faced with a stagnant meantime situation. Strong members of a family may start shrinking from decision and convictions. Even parents may try to reverse roles and turn to their children for help and guidance.

The person who emerges from a serious interim as the enabler of the family or group will be the one who realizes that someone must always take the daring step of leadership.

Too many families have been paralyzed by a crisis because everyone kept waiting for someone else to make the first move. There is an idealistic assumption in most families that everything is equal in family relationships, including responsibility. Again, we must remember that everyone is different, and being in a certain family does not necessarily equip everyone in the family with the same abilities.

Even love is not as equal as we would like to think. In *Where Angels Fear to Tread,* E. M. Forster wrote, "A wonderful physical tie binds the parents to the children; and—by some sad, strange irony—it does not bind us children to our parents. For if it did, if we could answer their love not with gratitude but with equal love, life might lose much of its pathos and much of its squalor, and we might be wonderfully happy."

It is difficult for most parents to realize that a child's love for parents is different from the parent's love for the child, but being realistic about this can set many parents free to act rather than waiting for the child to act. On the other hand, the child may be freer to act in more rational, less emotional ways than the parent who is more emotionally bound. The important thing is to remember that we are not all the same, even in our feelings toward each other, and that we cannot expect others to take the action we feel we should take.

We must not wait for someone else to come forward.

If we know what needs to be done, that very knowledge puts us in a responsible position. We can change the direction of the whole group by stating in a tactful but firm way that it's time for the next move. Even if others disagree with us, we will at least have started discussion and gotten off dead center. We must not be overly cautious during an interim lull. Inertia may be deadly to the family's relationships with each other. Action—even wrong action—keeps people thinking and changing. If we take creative control we can expect creative results.

3. *Family members must be clear about the essential nature of a family.* This is especially true in Judeo-Christian cultures. Misunderstanding about what a family really is will naturally cause problems when the strain of waiting sets in.

Elton Trueblood discussed three vital ingredients in the essential nature of marriage and family which are especially applicable to the family in transition. (These elements are treated at length in Trueblood's *The Recovery of Family Life,* pp. 43-57, *The Common Ventures of Life,* pp. 42-59, and *The Yoke of Christ,* pp. 182-192.) Trueblood said that the first essential of marriage is the acceptance of the relationship as unconditional. In the wedding ceremony the pledge was made "for better and for worse." True marriage is not a 50-50 agreement; it is a situation in which each gives *all* that he has. Marriage is not a bargain; it is uncalculating abandonment to the needs of the other.

This unrestricted, unconditional love applies to all aspects of family relationships. The father's responsibility to his child does not depend on the child's health, his success, or his character. Children are not kept from having shoes they need merely because they have not earned them. The mother may work far harder than any of the children, yet she may receive less than any in the division of family expenditure.

The family unit is not regulated by strict bookkeeping, with a careful balance between labor and reward. As Trueblood said, "The sacredness of the family lies in the fact that the basis of union is that of uncalculating affection."

During an interim tension there will be the temptation to place blame, to deny responsibility, to demand justice. The family needs to say to each other, "We're not keeping score on who is doing the most or least, the best or worst. We are loving and listening and supporting each other. We are, first and foremost, surviving together—all of us—as a family!"

Writing about his devastating experience in German concentration camps, Dr. Frankl said, "For the first time in my life I saw the truth as it is set into song by so many poets, proclaimed as the final wisdom by so many thinkers. The truth—that love is the ultimate and the highest goal to which man can aspire. Then I grasped the meaning of the greatest secret that human poetry and human thought and belief have to impart: The salvation of man is through love and in love."[3] Add to this splendid affirmation of love Dr. Trueblood's assertion that the basis for family union is an "uncalculating affection" and you have the formula for family survival—unconditional love.

Along this same line, Trueblood said that another distinctive feature of marriage and family is the free acceptance of a bond.

> The binding element is inherent in the family idea because without it, all the finer fruits of family love are impossible to produce. An unbinding marriage is no marriage at all. . . . Only those who have accepted

some bondage are really free. . . . Accepted bonds hold families together in spite of hard work, poverty, and much suffering. These accepted bonds make the family the one institution in which it is possible to say "we" without any loss of individuality.[4]

Trueblood conceded that the desire to escape family responsibilities is practically universal at some time or other, but then he reminded us of G. K. Chesterton's observation: "In everything on this earth that is worth doing, there is a stage when no one would do it except for necessity or honor."

Sometimes, especially during the pressure of waiting for things to work out, it seems it would be so nice to be free of responsibility. Many people do, in fact, yield to the lure of escape. They quit their jobs, leave their families, drop church, ignore bills that are due, and generally shrug off any bondage. But when they do, they cut themselves off from the richest and most meaningful relationships possible.

We should not curse the "bondage" of relationships during such struggles. We should rather thank God for them. These very bonds will keep us at the wheel until we have sailed around the rocks and are on the open sea again.

The other essential of family life, which Trueblood pointed out, is the public character of the family itself. He contended that true marriage cannot be strictly a private affair. The family contributes to the total good or ill of society. Influences that affect mankind in general come from individual homes. Children from any given home may be a burden or a strength to the outside community.

In ancient Israel, the family was understood as the

fundamental unit of the social order. When Jeremiah told the people in exile to keep the traditions of family alive he noted the purpose: "that ye may be increased there and not diminished." As the individual family went, so would the nation of Israel go. If they were to emerge a strong people, they needed to keep strong families during the interim.

At the council of Trent, Catholics reaffirmed the principle of *propries parochus,* meaning that, whenever possible, marriage is to be conducted in the parish where the couple live. The idea is that the judgment of local relatives, neighbors, and clergy should have an influence on the marriage. In standard Quaker practice, the couple intending marriage must seek the judgment of the local group at least a month before the ceremony. In *The Book of Church Order,* Presbyterians require that the intention of marriage be published "a proper time previous to the solemnization of it."

All of this is saying that the community has a stake in the new union and the results of this family. Marriage is so intrinsically sacred that it should receive the blessing of a group who care. All of us care about our reputations among those with whom we work and live. That may be one reason why divorce comes about so much more easily for people uprooted in a highly mobile society.

Our family may not be uprooted physically or geographically, but if we are having to endure a long uncertainty, we may be uprooted emotionally, mentally, socially, or financially.

We must try to keep as many roots in place as possible. One of the best ways is to maintain good relations with the community. People *do* care about what is happening to us. They may not know what to say, and they may not have any money to give, but they *do* care.

They may also be scared. If it can happen to us, it could happen to them. We must allow them to see that we and our families are carrying on as normally as possible. If they see us surviving, they will believe that they can too, if necessary.

We must keep our connections with the church, school, clubs, and friends. We must not become recluses, or be afraid of what the neighbor's children will say to ours. We must not expect people to shut us out or embarrass us. We must try to be as open and as involved as we would be in normal times.

Our families need community strength. We need to get outside ourselves and into the needs and activities of others. The community also needs our families. We have learned a lot from our experiences. They need our wisdom, strength, and assurance.

The English poet and clergyman John Donne wrote, "No man is an island, complete unto himself." In that same poem he remarked that when a clod is washed from the shores of England, England is that much less. We do belong to each other, and this sense of community can be both an affirmation and challenge in our meantimes.

So, let us look closely at our families. Let us see each person as an individual who deserves the chances of life. We must revive some neglected traditions and bring out some meaningful symbols. We must be honest about our own willingness to take the lead and to be vulnerable. We must make sure that the whole family understands that it is bound together in unrestricted commitment, freely accepted ties, and a sense of community oneness.

The best strength we can draw on for our trying days may be found not in external resources but in the deep wells of loving relationships already at work in our own family. Let us not waste the "acres of diamonds" in our own backyard.

5

Burying the Hatchet

And seek the peace of the city whither I have caused you to be carried away captives, and pray unto the Lord for it: for in the peace thereof shall ye have peace (Jeremiah 29:7).

Bitterness and anger are normal human emotions when one has been hurt deeply. Many of the meantimes we have to endure come about because someone has destroyed our dreams, broken our hearts, or thwarted our plans. It is bad enough to be put on hold and have to wait for relief, but it is an additional burden to carry resentment and hatred during the waiting period. We can't escape all the problems or shrug off all the burdens of our meantime, but we can get rid of the crippling weight of bitterness and be free from the blinding disease of hatred.

However, we usually don't want to give up our negative feelings toward an enemy or someone who has hurt us. Anger and hatred have an energizing force that gives motivation, direction, and power. We are often our strongest when we are our meanest. But we need to realize that this apparent force or power has a singular direction; it is self-destructive. All the hostility we feel and express to others does more damage to us than it does to them. If we cannot get free from it, we will eventually destroy ourselves.

The Israelite exiles were consumed with hatred for their Babylonian captors. These pagan enemies had besieged, overthrown, and ravaged their beloved Jerusalem. The temple had been destroyed, the city razed to the ground, crops burned and families shattered. Men, women, and children had been slaughtered like cattle, and the captive exiles had been torn from the bleeding arms of loved ones.

In a stupor of grief and blinding hatred, the exiles refused to entertain their captors: "They that carried us away captive required of us a song; and they that wasted us required of us mirth, saying, Sing us one of the songs of Zion. How shall we sing the Lord's song in a strange land?" (Psalm 137:3, 4).

This familiar and plaintive psalm from the exile does not end with verse 4 where we usually end our reading. The psalmist, speaking for exiled Israel, went on to vow that he would never forget his beloved and desecrated Jerusalem (vv. 5, 6). Then he called on Jehovah to remember that the Babylonians had deliberately and gleefully destroyed Jerusalem, chanting, "Raze it, raze it, even to the foundations thereof" (v. 7). Finally, the embittered psalmist cried out for Babylon to be treated the same way as Jerusalem (v. 8), even to the point of pronouncing blessing upon those who would dash Babylonian infants against the stones as the Israelite infants had been so slaughtered (v. 9).

We are shocked and bewildered by this overwhelming spirit of vindictiveness in the psalmist. With our New Testament standards of mercy and forgiveness, it is difficult to understand, let alone accept, this Old Testament attitude.

While it is true that this was a prevalent Old Testament attitude toward one's enemies, we should not jump to the conclusion that it was God's attitude. God does not change, and the God of the Jews in the Old Testament is the same God of Jesus in the New Testament. Our interpretation of God may change, but God himself does not.

Also, we need to understand that everything recorded in sacred Scripture does not reflect God's spirit. The skeptics in Job and the cynic in Ecclesiastes express philosophies which are incompatible with the Christian view of God, and the psalmist of the exile ventilated his hatred against the Babylonians in the psalm recorded in the Bible, but his attitude toward Babylon was not God's attitude.

We need to be very careful in our lives at this point. An attitude of vengeance may seem logically justified and personally acceptable to us. Our friends may even agree that we have a right to feel as we do, but that does not mean that it is God's attitude or has God's approval.

God revealed his attitude in Jeremiah's letter to the exiles. They must have been aghast at the suggestion, in fact, the commandment, to pray for their enemies: "And seek the peace of the city whither I have caused you to be carried away captives, and pray unto the Lord for it; for in the peace thereof shall ye have peace."

Pray for Babylon? Pray for its welfare? Pray for it to have peace and prosperity? Pray for these murderers, rapists, looters, and pagans? Pray *for* them? We can easily pray *against* them, as the psalmist had done, but how can we possibly pray *for* them?

We can readily identify with the doubting exiles. They couldn't believe that their God would expect such a hard thing from them. We also have difficulty believing that God really expects us to forgive and pray for those who have wreaked havoc in our lives.

Yet we have to admit that we are haunted by the soft, insistent words of Jesus: "Love your enemies, bless them that curse you, and pray for them which despitefully use you, and persecute you" (Matthew 5:44). This is the same Jesus who taught us to pray, "Forgive us our debts, as we also have forgiven our debtors," because "if you do not forgive men their sins, your Father will not forgive your sins" (Matthew 6:12, 15, NIV).

The God of Jeremiah and God the Son—Jesus—is the same God. He who required the Israelites to forgive and pray for the Babylonians also requires us to forgive and pray for our enemies.

It takes courage to do that. For some strange reason we are afraid to turn loose of our hatred, and it takes divine courage to do it. In *Thor, With Angels,* Christopher Fry wrote:

> What shall we do? We are afraid
> To live by rule of God, which is forgiveness,
> Mercy, and compassion, fearing that by these
> We shall be ended. And yet if we could bear
> These three through dread and terrors' doubt,
> Daring to return good for evil without thought
> Of what will come, I cannot think
> We should be the losers. Do we believe
> There is no strength in good or power in God?
> God give us courage to exist in God,
> And lonely flesh be welcome to creation.

According to Fry, "courage to exist in God" is "to live by the rule of God, which is forgiveness, mercy, and compassion." All of us want to live by "the rule of God," but we need help to do it when all our natural instincts turn us in the other direction.

In Maxwell Anderson's *Winterset,* Mio begged his beloved Miriamne to help free him from a consuming desire to revenge himself upon those who permitted his innocent father to be executed. He was weary of dragging his hatred around and was horrified to see how it was affecting Miriamne. He said to her:

I've lost my taste for revenge
if it falls on you. Oh, God,
deliver me from the body of
this death I've dragged behind
me all these years!
Miriamne, if you love me
teach me a treason to what I am,
and have been, till I learn
to live like a man! I think
I'm waking from a long
trauma of hate and fear and death
that's hemmed me from my birth—
and glimpse a life to be lived in hope—
but it's young in me yet, I can't
get free, or forgive! But teach me
how to live and forget to hate!
I've groped long enough through
this everglades of old revenges—
here the road ends.

Several years ago I experienced the agony of Mio's groping through old revenges. I was serving as associate pastor on a large church staff when I was suddenly betrayed by friends and undercut by the one person who could have saved me. Although I was completely exonerated by the personnel committee, the damage had been done and to avoid a full church fight I offered my resignation. With a wife and two small children, I trudged through a long meantime of unemployment and fear. For five months we had no work and no hope. Then, God moved with a strong hand and put me in the pastorate of one of the finest churches in our state. During the interim of waiting and praying, I was filled with bitterness that bordered on raw hatred. I could not understand why God would let the guilty off and allow the innocent to suffer. I had horrible nightmares depicting violent vengeance against the man who had almost destroyed me.

Even when I got back into the ministry the nightmares would not cease and, like Mio, I continued to drag the death of my hatred behind me. My church work was suffering because of my attitude. I could not bring myself to trust anyone. I was suspicious, selfish, and defensive at every turn. I could not live in the present because I could not forget and forgive the past.

Finally, I was sick of it. I wanted nothing more to do with vengeance and reprisal. I wanted my heart back again. I remember exactly where I was the moment I gave my bitterness to God and asked him to please take it away. I could almost feel it lifting physically off my shoulders and floating upward. I felt clean and free and knew the first peace I had known in more than a year.

Sooner or later, the bitter, hurting soul has to say with Mio, "I've groped long enough through this everglades of old revenges—here the road ends."

One reason I came to the end of my vengeance road was because I was faced with the same opportunity and temptation to hurt one of my associates as I had been hurt. I was rudely shaken to realize how close I had come to being like the man I hated for betraying me. Then I remembered the words of Mrs. Macauley in William Saroyan's *The Human Comedy:*

> The evil man must be forgiven every day. He must be loved, because something of each of us is in the most evil man in the world and something of him is in each of us. He is ours and we are his. None of us is separate from any other. The peasant's prayer is my prayer, the assassin's crime is my crime.

The burden of guilt is not always so one-sided as we would like to think. Good guys don't always wear white hats and bad guys don't always wear black hats. In *The Deadly Game,* Friedrich Duerrenmatt reminded us:

> In this world of ours no one is completely innocent. Each of us carries some burden of guilt which troubles him and fills him with self-loathing. Where would sympathy, mercy, forgiveness come from if not from our common share of fallibility?

Viktor Frankl said that his relationships with both the prisoners and the guards in the concentration camp taught him that

> there are two races of men in this world, but only these two—the "race" of the decent man and the "race" of the indecent man. Both are found everywhere; they penetrate into all groups of society. No group consists entirely of decent or indecent people. In this sense, no group is of "pure race"—and therefore one occasionally found a decent fellow among the camp guards.[1]

In time, the Israelite exiles began to see that they were not so different from the Babylonians as they had thought. They began to see their captors as human beings, with the same human weaknesses and strengths that they themselves possessed. Perhaps they began to ask themselves honestly what they would have done to the Babylonians if they had been victors instead of victims. They could remember that their own record concerning mercy was not very clean, especially during the conquest of Canaan under Joshua. But, more than anything, these family-oriented Jews saw that Babylonians also had families they loved.

In Erich Maria Remarque's *All Quiet on the Western Front*, Paul Baumer cried out to the enemy soldier he had just killed:

Comrade, I did not want to kill you. If you jumped in here again, I would not do it, if you would be sensible too. But you were only an idea to me before, an abstraction that lived in my mind and called forth its appropriate response. It was that abstraction I stabbed. But, now, for the first time, I see you are a man like me. I thought of your hand grenades, of your bayonet, of your rifle; now I see your wife and your face and fellowships. Forgive me, comrade. We always see it too late. Why do they never tell us that you are just poor devils like us, that your mothers are just as anxious as ours, and that we have the same fear of death, and the same dying and the same agony—forgive me, comrade; how could you be my enemy?

And this was Jeremiah's question to the exiles: How can the Babylonians be your enemies now for you share the same city and the same destiny? "Pray for the peace of this city for in its peace you will find peace."

When we finally comprehend that we all share the same city, the same pilgrimage, the same fears and dreams and hopes, then perhaps we can pray *for* each other rather than *against* each other.

Then a strange and lovely transformation takes place. The peace, for which we pray for our enemy becomes our peace. The welfare we seek for our adversary becomes our own blessing. We cannot give without receiving. We cast our bread on the waters and it comes back a hundredfold.

This reciprocity in forgiveness and mercy forms one of the strongest bonds in human relationships. Bitterest enemies, when reconciled, become the fastest of friends. The community of forgiveness is the most endearing fellowship to which we can belong.

In *Time and Time Again,* James Hilton wrote: "If you

forgive people enough you belong to them, and they to you, whether either person likes it or not . . . the squatter's rights of the heart."

This was what Jeremiah was calling for Israel to do, to set up "the squatter's rights of the heart." They gained their squatter's rights in Babylon by forgiveness not by force. They finally accepted the fact that they must make peace and in so doing made a peace for themselves in an alien land.

When Carlyle Marney came to this portion of Jeremiah's letter, he spelled out how hard it was for the Jews to do it, but how crucial for their very survival.

> And in the meantime—now comes Jeremiah's most shocking and heretical statement to these Jerualem-loving Jews, heartsick for their native streets and haunts. It is heresy; it is treason; but while they are kept from their Jerusalem, says the Lord: "Seek the welfare of the city where I have sent you into exile, and pray to the Lord on its behalf."
>
> This is hard to take. Loving Jerusalem, aching to return, held captive in Babylon, they are to learn to love their place of exile—to seek the peace of the city where they are captive. And *pray* for it.
>
> That is to say, with Alfred Whitehead, "It is a mistake to cling to a region through which one has already passed." Man must put down some roots where he is. There is a need in Babylon, he must seek the peace of the city where he is.
>
> What if the only peace a person gets is Babylon's kind of peace? What if the years of his captivity swept over him and washed him away until he had no chance for peace except the peace he could have had in Babylon where he is? What if what he now has with his own in this place is all he gets?
>
> The Lord through Jeremiah says the Jews had better take their peace now: "for in its welfare [of Babylon, that is] you will find your welfare."

> They have a return on their investment, he says. The welfare of Babylon *is* their welfare, the only welfare they get, where they are. Their recovery from meantime rests on their making Babylon peaceful. Babylon is home, and in Babylon's welfare is the welfare of all.[2]

Of course, one does not have to pray for his enemies nor seek the peace of Babylon. We can continue to hold grudges, harbor resentment, express anger, and plot for vengeance. But our meantime, however long, will be wasted in fruitless emotions, and our friends and family will be poisoned with our spirit. But, more important than all, God himself will be blotted out by our dark testimony. Christ will lose the bright witness of our mercy and forgiveness. For our own sake, for our loved ones' sake, for our enemy's sake, but especially for Christ's sake, we must give up the long battle for vengeance and turn loose of the weapon of anger.

A beautiful incident occurred in *The Great Hunger,* by Johan Bojer, which eloquently calls us all to pray for our Babylonian enemies. Peer Holms was a simple farmer whose little daughter was killed by his neighbor's dog. Peer's friends stood by him in his grief. They all refused to sell seed to his neighbor or in any way help this one who had been responsible for the tragedy. But, early one morning Peer crossed over and sowed corn in his neighbor's field. He explained the reason for his curious deed: "Mankind must arrive, and be better than the blind powers that order its ways; in the midst of its sorrows it must take heed that the god-like does not die. The spark of eternity was once more aglow in me, and said: Let there be light. . . . Therefore I went out and sowed the corn in my enemy's field, that God might exist."

When Jeremiah told the exiles to marry and carry on

their families he said that it was in order for Israel to live. When he told them to pray for Babylon, he was calling on them to let God live.

The Apostle Paul echoed Jeremiah's call centuries later: "Do not take revenge, my friends, but leave room for God's wrath, for it is written: 'It is mine to avenge; I will repay,' says the Lord. On the contrary: 'If your enemy is hungry, feed him; if he is thirsty, give him something to drink. In doing this, you will heap burning coals on his head.' Do not be overcome by evil, but overcome evil with good" (Romans 12:19-21, NIV).

A professor in our local university told me about his victory over resentment toward his immediate superior who was constantly harassing him. Taking creative control, the professor began to put their offices in order and to arrange things for the convenience of his superior. He said, "As soon as my task was done, the burden of resentment was gone. The poison was gone and I've been singing ever since. I told a friend what I had done, and she responded by declaring that she was going to make an apple pie for her mother-in-law whom she had trouble loving. Again it worked."

We do not have to perform some great deed to put things right between us and another. A very simple action can convey the message. But we must do something; we can't sit and wait for things to "work themselves out." Paul's exhortation was to "overcome evil with good!" This is not passive weakness; this is active strength. We must deliberately and courageously take the initiative and conquer our enemies by making them our friends.

6

Rejecting False Hope

Let not your prophets and your diviners, that be in the midst of you, deceive you, neither hearken to your dreams which ye cause to be dreamed. For they prophesy falsely unto you in my name: I have not sent them, saith the Lord. (Jeremiah 29:8, 9).

Meantime crises have a way of producing prophets of hope. Most of them are well-meaning and harmless. They express their assurances in worn clichés: "Cheer up! Chin up! Look up! It's always darkest before the dawn. Things will work out. You're looking great. We're all pulling for you. It could be worse. God won't let you down." They really want to help. They really mean to be positive. They just don't have much creativity or depth in their expressions.

But, then, there are other prophets of hope who try to capitalize on the troubles of others. Like so-called "ambulance chasers," they are out to make some kind of profit out of your tragedy. As soon as they see an accident, they "chase the ambulance" to sell a service or product to the hapless victim.

Sometimes the self-appointed prophets step in to make themselves look good or to get the credit when things go as they predicted. They want the world to know it was they who healed us, or prayed for us, or cheered us on, or stood by us. They use our temporary invalidism to make themselves look strong.

Of course, sometimes the prophets of hope are passionately sincere. They refuse to believe that evil can triumph. They "accentuate the positive and eliminate the negative" in the face of undeniable facts. They see everything through rose-colored glasses. They cannot allow us to succumb to despair or they might become vulnerable themselves. They know what the right outcome should be and earnestly believe that right thinking and positive praying will make everything turn out right.

There are many reasons why people emerge during our meantime nightmare to give us advice, encouragement, and hope. For the sake of our mental health, spiritual posture, and vital decisions we must learn to discern the true prophets from the false prophets. We need to be able to recognize a bogus message when we hear it, but we don't want to close our ears to the truth when it is spoken.

The exiles in Babylon were inundated with false prophets, who kept telling the Israelites that they would soon be back home. They promised relief that never came. They told the people that their dreams of Jerusalem were God's messages of promise. They knew how desperately the exiles wanted to believe, so they ingratiated themselves to the people by telling them what they wanted to hear.

Today we are all familiar with quack doctors and pseudo-faith healers who give false hope to desperate people who are willing to grasp at any straw. Viktor Frankl said, "In psychiatry there is a certain condition known as 'delusion of reprieve.' The condemned man, immediately before his execution, gets the illusion that he might be reprieved at the very last moment."

False prophets deliberately feed on this phenomenon, taking advantage of the victims of depression or disease. But, sincere and honest friends also can unknowingly contribute to the delusion by being overly optimistic. For a while people are cheered by positive thoughts, but soon they begin to want honest and straightforward reports.

Frankl wrote, "Many times, hopes for a speedy end to the war, which had been fanned by optimistic rumors, were disappointed. Some men lost hope, but it was the incorrigible optimists who were the most irritating companions."[1]

Now, the important question for us in our meantime is how to know the difference between false hope and real hope. We want to have faith and be positive, but we also want to be honest and realistic. True hope must not be built on ignorance or dishonesty, just as true science cannot develop without honesty about the facts of nature.

The familiar story of Galileo trying to get the churchmen of his day to see what he had discovered about the universe was portrayed in Horsanyi's *The Star-Gazer*. In one scene Galileo is imploring a theologian friend to look through his telescope. The friend retorted, "Listen, Galileo! The science of the world was built on the pillars of Aristotelian wisdom. For two thousand years men have lived and died in the belief that the earth is the center of the universe and man the lord of it. . . . Leave me my peace of mind! I refuse to look into that tube!"

Galileo replied, "But the truth, Cesare! The truth! Doesn't that mean anything? To me peace and happiness have always meant one thing: to seek truth and admit what I found."

Most of us would affirm that we also want nothing but the truth, but in reality we want the truth to be good news about our situation. How can we have both truth and good news?

As we turn again to the biblical narrative which furnishes the background for this book, we find Jeremiah demonstrating the posture of both truth and hope. He was certain of God's eventual deliverance, but he was unalterably opposed to the false message of immediate relief.

Jeremiah had to confront false prophets in both Jerusalem and Babylon. Hananiah, a Jerusalemite prophet from Gibeon, spoke to Jeremiah in the temple, disagreeing with his insistence that Judah should live under Babylonian domination (Jeremiah 28:1-17). Hananiah said that within two years of Jerusalem's first surrender the vessels taken from the temple would be returned and Jeconiah and all the exiles would return. He declared that the Lord would "break the yoke of the king of Babylon." To emphasize his point, he broke the yoke which Jeremiah wore to symbolize submission to Nebuchadnezzar.

Several features of Jeremiah's response furnish us a formula for discerning between true and false hope. First, Jeremiah agreed with the intent of Hananiah's prophecy (v. 6). In effect, he said, "Amen, brother Hananiah, I pray with all my heart you are right. I want God to bring our people back as much as you do." This reflected a genuine spirit of concern. Jeremiah wished that he was wrong and Hananiah was right; his main concern was for the plight of the exiles. This was the sign of a true prophet.

False prophets must always be right; they must be vindicated. Their main interest is in looking good, not doing good. They do not rejoice when God chooses some other method than the one they espoused. True prophets are willing to let God be God if they are proven wrong. False prophets refuse to admit they were wrong regardless of the outcome.

When I was diagnosed as having multiple sclerosis

and went through an interminable dark meantime, many good people prayed for my healing, but a few were determined to force their own brand of faith healing on me. One friend even traveled several hundred miles to "heal me."

In the dramatic turn of events, we discovered that I did not have MS, but instead I had five herniated discs, which were corrected by surgery. Family, friends, and fellow Christians everywhere rejoiced with the good news and my eventual recovery to full health. However, not one single person who had insisted on healing me miraculously, including the friend who had traveled so far, has to this day spoken one word to me about how glad they are that God did such a beautiful thing for me. In fact, some of the would-be healers became angry and left our church when I let the doctors operate instead of letting them "heal" me.

The kind, loving spirit of Jeremiah was willing to be wrong for Israel's sake. The spirit of our friends will help reveal the validity of their message. Do they really want what is best for us, or are they determined to prove they are right, even at our expense?

The second thing Jeremiah replied to Hananiah was that any prophecy of peace should wait for its fulfillment before people assessed its validity (v. 9). Jeremiah was applying the old adage, "time will tell." We should always be suspicious of do-gooders and soothsayers who want instant acceptance. Any honest person is willing to wait for the test of time. Those who insist strongly and loudly that you buy their offerings immediately should be held at arm's length.

In *White Banners,* Lloyd C. Douglas had Hannah declare, "I claim that anybody who really is right and honest can live his whole lifetime without ever raising his voice above the tone of ordinary conversation. When the Truth begins to screech and whack the desk with its fist, it always makes me think of Little Red Ridinghood's long-eared grandmother."

Jeremiah's third reaction was to wait patiently for God's next word to him: "Shortly after, the word of the Lord came to Jeremiah" (v. 12, NIV). The prophet did not claim automatic access to God's Word; he had to wait for its revelation. Jeremiah did not try to withdraw an inspired message in the face of criticism. He was willing to wait.

False prophets always have a word. They have an opinion, a diagnosis, and a prognosis on every ailment. They don't have to wait for second opinions or divine revelations. They somehow feel uniquely equipped to describe and prescribe. They often disagree with doctors, psychiatrists, and theologians. We should be very cautious about those who tell us to ignore the counsel of reputable professionals.

I have much more confidence in the person who compassionately and honestly says, "I just don't know," than I do in the one who always knows the answer. I trust the strong, silent type who says we must wait, we must have more evidence, we must not jump to conclusions.

Jeremiah said, "I don't have an answer for Hananiah right now, but if and when the Lord gives it to me, I'll pass it on." Jeremiah continued to be the spokesman for God for many years to come; Hananiah died within the year.

There were also prophets in Babylon who disagreed with Jeremiah's message of Babylonian domination. They hoped for a brief period of exile, contrary to Jeremiah's predicted seventy years. Concerning those prophets who had gone down with the exiles to Babylon, Jeremiah warned, "Do not let the prophets and diviners among you deceive you . . . They are prophesying lies" (29:8, 9, NIV).

At least two of these false prophets are named in verse 21, Ahab and Zedekiah. They minimized the crisis while exploiting the situation. They were not only dishonest, they were also immoral and self-indulgent (v. 23). They flagrantly tried to turn Israel's plight to their own advantage and pleasure.

While we should not be cynical nor overly-suspicious of people, it is always in order to know why someone is taking a special interest in our situation. Do they have something to gain by our misfortune? Are they taking advantage of our weakened position? Are we allowing them privileges we would not under normal circumstances? Are we listening to them because they say what we want to hear, whether it's true or not?

We often wonder how false prophets continue to be successful. Yet, it is our own human nature that feeds their success. Kenneth Roberts wrote in *Oliver Wiswell,* "Great men tell the truth and are never believed. Lesser men are always believed, but seldom have the brains or the courage to tell the truth."

Jeremiah recognized the human tendency to believe what we want to believe. He also realized that people will try to blot out the facts of the real world by turning to the fantasies of a dream world: "Do not hearken to your dreams which you cause to be dreamed." We create our own world in our imagination of what things could or should be like, instead of accepting the reality of things.

Hope that has any possibility of coming true must be based on reality, not dreams. I believe there are enough wonderful, positive facts in our world to give hope in almost any situation. We do not have to create a Utopia or fantasize a miracle. We can participate in the creative and positive forces already at work in our world and our circumstances.

In *The Black Rose,* Thomas B. Costain wrote:

> Truth lies all about us: in the air we breathe, in the life that pulses around us, in the natural laws that govern our simplest actions. We do not reach an understanding of nature's laws by the mumbling of spells and incantations. We can reach them only by watching and by winnowing truth and reason from what we see.

One final observation about Jeremiah's confrontation with the false prophets is his emphasis on judgment. The false prophets looked for the quick overthrow of Babylon, and did not include judgment in their message to Judah. Jeremiah said that God's plans involve not only hope for the future, but that the travail of judgment and the reality of repentance were required for renewal (29:15-19).

Israel had repeatedly rebelled against God. Even in captivity the people rejected his true message and hearkened to false prophets. God said that he could not take them home again until he had purged them. They needed to face the consequences of their rebellion and pay for their sins. Deliverance could come only after judgment and repentance.

There is a message here for all of us who want everything to be back like it was without having to pay the price for our mistakes. Not all of our meantimes are brought about by our mistakes or sins, but many of them are. Personally, I know that most of my dark nights of waiting were caused by my own decisions or mistakes. And, since we live in a world of cause and effect, I have had to live with many of the effects I have caused. Once we have chosen a path, we must follow it through, including all the pitfalls, detours, and dangers.

Paul said, "Do not be deceived: God cannot be mocked. A man reaps what he sows" (Galatians 6:7, NIV). James reminded us of nature's law of the harvest when he said, "Can a fig tree bear olives or a grapevine bear figs? Neither can a salt spring produce fresh water" (James 3:12, NIV).

False hope ignores the law of the harvest, seeks to bypass consequences of mistakes, and prays that judgment will be withheld. True hope acknowledges the law of the harvest, accepts the consequences of mistakes, and knows that judgment is inevitable. Where is hope in that? It is there because we can hope only if we are honest. We can only be restored if we are purged. We can only be redeemed if we have accepted judgment. We can escape future mistakes only when we confess to and accept the consequences of past mistakes.

"But, isn't this dangerous?" you ask. "Isn't this making yourself vulnerable? Isn't this asking for heartache and trouble? Wouldn't it be better to keep believing that you deserve the best and are going to get the best?"

That is a matter of opinion, of course, but I happen to believe that honesty and reality and the law of the harvest hold out the best hope for us. I hear Jeremiah saying the same thing. Only when we are willing to be open and vulnerable can real hope and joy come. We have to take the chance of failure before we can succeed. We have to be willing to be unhappy before we can know what happiness is.

In Aldous Huxley's *Brave New World*, it was six hundred years A. F. (after Ford) and Science was offering mankind relief from every conceivable agony of mind and spirit. The World Controller said to John, a savage, "We prefer to do things comfortably." John protested, "But I don't want comfort. I want God, I want poetry, I want real danger, I want freedom, I want goodness, I want sin." The World Controller replied, "In fact, you're claiming the right to be unhappy." John answered, "All right then, I'm claiming the right to be unhappy."

If all we want is to be comfortable and "happy" we can accept all the false hope that people offer. But if we are willing to be unhappy for the sake of authentic life and willing to be uncomfortable for the sake of truth, we can build a strong hope on the facts and our willingness to face them.

Viktor Frankl recounted that in his quiet talks with his fellow prisoners he urged them to open their eyes to reality in order to open their hearts to hope.

> I told my comrades that human life, under any circumstances, never ceases to have a meaning, and that this infinite meaning of life includes suffering and dying, privation and death. I asked the poor creatures who listened to me attentively in the darkness of the hut to face up to the seriousness of our position. They must not lose hope but should keep their courage in the certainty that the hopelessness of our struggle did not detract from its dignity and meaning.[2]

And there can be dignity and meaning in our struggle if we will face up to the seriousness of our position and base our hope on truth and justice.

7

Praying and Seeking a Way Out

Then shall ye call upon me, and ye shall go and pray unto me, and I will hearken unto you. And ye shall seek me, and find me, when ye shall search for me with all your heart (Jeremiah 29:12, 13).

Our physical possibilities appear to be exhausted and our spiritual resources seem to be powerless. We have prayed and prayed, but can't seem to get through to God. Everytime we share our burden and some well-meaning friend says, "You must pray and trust the Lord," we feel like screaming, "What do you think I've been doing? Every waking moment I have been pleading with God. I have prayed and begged and confessed and promised until I'm just simply 'prayed out.' "

We feel that the heroine of Mary Borden's *Jane—Our Stranger* expressed our own frustration when she said, "It would have been an immense relief to me to have known that God was in His Heaven. . . . I used to try talking to God, but praying was like whispering into a chasm, a void, an echoing emptiness. My questions came back to me, unanswered, mocking echoes of my tormented soul."

Some of us have felt that way. Some of us may feel that way now, in the midst of our meantime waiting. What's the use of praying if things stay the same? Is God really interested in the entanglements of our lives? The problem of unanswered prayer is the most perplexing aspect of most situations. Until we find peace about prayer it is doubtful we will feel right about most other parts of our problems.

The exiles in Babylon were devout Jews. They were a deeply religious people and prayer was an integral part of their religion. They must have been thoroughly confused by the seeming impotence of their prayers. Where was the God of Abraham, Jacob, Moses, David and all the prophets? They had been told again and again to pray unto the God of their fathers, but that God seemed to have closed his ears to their cries.

Was it possible that these Israelites needed to learn something new about prayer? Most people probably think there is nothing new to be said or heard about prayer. We simply tell God what we want and he either gives it to us or he doesn't.

Well, it really isn't that simple. Prayer is a continually growing, changing, revealing aspect of our relationship with God. Even though I have a Ph.D. in theology, have taught college, pastored for many years, and have even written a book about prayer, I often feel that I am just beginning kindergarten in the school of prayer. Almost every day brings to light a new element of praying, and I am constantly learning from others how to communicate with God. So, even though we may feel that we have prayed adequately and wisely, we need to try one more time to learn a new approach to God or to practice a new posture of faith in prayer.

Jeremiah called upon his fellow countrymen to pray, and certain aspects of his call to prayer provoke creative thinking about prayer itself.

In the first place, Jeremiah put prayer in a significant position in the process of deliverance. Chapter 29 of Jeremiah is an unfolding sequence of things to be done in our meantime situations. These include: accepting the reality of things (vv. 1-3), seeing God behind the scenes

(vv. 4, 11), getting back to work (v. 5), considering the family (v. 6), burying the hatchet (v. 7), rejecting false hope (vv. 8, 9), and *then* comes praying and seeking (vv. 12, 13).

In fact, Jeremiah began verse 12 with the word "then." The word "then" always implies an antecedent. Something else has gone before. After these other things have been done, "*then* shall ye pray unto me and I will hearken unto you."

I am not suggesting that we should not even start to pray until all things have been put in order. Certainly not, for the Scriptures tell us to pray without ceasing, morning, noon, and night. We should not let a day of this interim drag by without bathing it in prayer.

But prayer must be seen as only one part of the natural process in our relationship with God, and in the working out of our problems. Prayer is not magic that ignores facts and changes things and people like we want them to be. Prayer will not automatically undo damage we have caused or perform deeds that are our responsibility. Prayer does not erase reality; instead it opens up possibilities of a new reality in which you can participate. Prayer cannot change the past, but it can dramatically shape the future.

In Richard Llewellyn's *How Green Was My Valley,* Mr. Gruffydd said, "Prayer is not mumbling, or shouting, or wallowing like a hog in religious sentiments. Prayer is only another name for good, clean, direct thinking."

Therefore, before we pray and ask God to do something, we should honestly ask ourselves if we have done everything we can. We must practice "good, clean, direct thinking" about ourselves, our situation, and realistic options.

Next, we should notice that Jeremiah's call to prayer is divided into two distinct types of praying. One is asking and receiving (v. 12) and the other is seeking and finding (v. 13). Doesn't that sound like Jesus' teaching on prayer? "So I say to you: Ask and it will be given to you; seek and you will find. . . . for everyone who asks receives; and he who seeks finds" (Luke 11:9, 10, NIV). In my book, *How to Get What You Pray For,*[1] I suggest that these words of Jesus imply two different kinds of prayer answers: received answers and found answers.

Asking and receiving go hand in hand just as do seeking and finding. Achieving is one thing, but receiving is quite another. Achieving is something I can do. Receiving means accepting what someone else has done. Both achieving and receiving have their legitimate place in the Christian life. It will help clear up a lot of questions when we learn to keep the distinction between achieving and receiving.

For instance, salvation comes by receiving the grace of God, not by the achievement of good works (Ephesians 2:8, 9). But fulfilling God's intention for our lives is achieved by the doing of his will (Ephesians 2:10). We achieve growth and maturity here on earth, but we receive eternal life as his gift (Romans 6:23).

We achieve many good things in this life because we have worked for them and earned them, and that is as it should be. In fact, I am one who doubts that we ought to ask God for anything we can honorably achieve for ourselves.

There are, however, many things which we can receive only through direct answer to prayer. Receiving straight from God things we cannot achieve for ourselves is a very distinct kind of answer, which harmonizes with the teachings of Christ.

Immediately following his exhortation about asking, seeking, and knocking, Jesus said, "Your heavenly Father [will] give the Holy Spirit to them that ask him" (Luke 11:13). This is something we cannot achieve for ourselves. The indwelling Christ comes to those who ask him to come in. Paul specifically related salvation also to prayer: "For whosoever shall call upon the name of the Lord shall be saved" (Romans 10:13).

Knowledge is something we can achieve through study and observation, but spiritual wisdom or discernment can be received only from God. "If any of you lacks wisdom, he should ask God, who gives generously to all without finding fault, and it will be given to him" (James 1:5, NIV).

The supporting presence of God in trouble is something we cannot work up; we receive it with a trusting heart: "He will call upon me, and I will answer him; I will be with him in trouble, I will deliver him and honor him" (Psalm 91:15, NIV). "Then you will call, . . . and he will say: Here am I" (Isaiah 58:9, NIV).

Receiving a special enduement to turn tragedy into triumph is definitely a grace gift from God: "This third I will bring into the fire; I will refine them like silver and test them like gold. They will call on my name and I will answer them" (Zechariah 13:9, NIV).

Forgiveness of sins cannot be achieved by doing penance or earning merits of righteousness but only by receiving his gracious response to our prayer of confession: "If we confess our sins, he is faithful and just and will forgive us our sins and purify us from all unrighteousness" (1 John 1:9, NIV).

In the Sermon on the Mount, Jesus spoke about our creaturely needs such as clothing and food, reminding us that our "heavenly Father knows that you need them"

(Matthew 6:32). Then he instructed us to "seek first his kingdom and his righteousness, and all these things will be given to you as well" (6:33, NIV).

After we have done all that we can and should in our responsibility as children of God, we can trust the heavenly Father to provide our necessities. But, there are special things for which we pray because no one but God can do them. Asking and receiving become a very conscious reality to us.

In *Aurora Leigh,* Elizabeth Barrett Browning reminded us that

> God answers sharp and sudden on
>   some prayers,
> And thrusts the thing we have prayed for
>   in our face,
> A gauntlet with a gift in 't.

Everything we have comes from God: "Every good gift and every perfect gift is from above, and cometh down from the Father of lights" (James 1:17). But, the Bible's teachings on prayer seem to indicate that there are special blessings beyond our common provisions which are available to those who ask for them. Another passage from James is: "You do not have, because you do not ask God" (James 4:2, NIV).

A frequent question about prayer is, "Why do I need to pray if God already knows what I need and want?" This is a logical question, because Jesus did indeed say, "Your Father knoweth what things ye have need of, before ye ask him" (Matthew 6:8).

We do not know why God tells us to pray for what he already knows we need. But we do know that he tells us to. The dedicated disciple obeys because the Master has spoken, not because he understands or agrees with the Master. Stonewall Jackson once said, "My duty is to obey orders." So it should be with the soldiers of the cross.

Jesus was always trying to get people to communicate with him, to tell their deepest longings. It seemed as though he was holding something special for those who would ask. These thoughts remind me of the famous lines from James Russell Lowell:

> For a cap and bells our lives we pay,
> Bubbles we buy with the whole soul's tasking:
> Tis heaven alone is given away,
> Tis only God may be had for the asking.

The second part of Jeremiah's admonition called for seeking along with praying. In fact, I believe that seeking is itself a very real kind of prayer. That is why I speak of received answers and found answers. Received answers are those sent directly from God which we cannot achieve or merit. Found answers are those which we discover, but they are still to be thought of as answers from God. We could not find them if God had not placed them in the world for our discovery and if he had not given us the desire to seek.

So, in our praying, we should try to anticipate answers that are either received or achieved and pray accordingly. We must remember also that too many people stop at Jesus' first words on prayer: "Ask and ye shall receive." That is all they hear and all they really want to hear. To them, praying is their part and giving is God's part. They sit, waiting for God to supply their needs. There are, indeed many prayer answers that are received answers, but there is also a legitimate place in our prayer life for found answers.

Jesus said, "Seek and you will find" in the specific context of teaching about prayer. His disciples said, "Lord, teach us to pray" (Luke 11:1). In response, Jesus taught them the Lord's Prayer (vv. 2-4). Following that, he told the story of the friend who came at midnight, illustrating persistency in prayer (vv. 5-8). In the following verses we read about the heavenly Father who gives good gifts to his children who pray. In the midst of all this comes the "ask, seek, and knock" passage (vv. 8-10).

So, the admonition to "seek and find" is not related here to intellectual pursuits or treasure hunts. It is an integrated part of the prayer process. Getting what we pray for often depends on our seeking and finding, just as it sometimes means asking and receiving.

The Bible repeatedly instructs us to seek God, who is the source and ground of all that we pray for. As Moses was preparing the people to enter the promised land of Canaan, he said, "If from there you seek the Lord your God, you will find him if you look for him with all your heart and with all your soul" (Deuteronomy 4:29, NIV).

Centuries later, settled in the conquered land, the descendants of Moses' followers heard their shepherd-king David repeat the same exhortation, "Seek the Lord, and his strength: seek his face evermore" (Psalm 105:4).

Then came the clarion call of the prophet Isaiah, "Seek ye the Lord while he may be found, call ye upon him while he is near" (Isaiah 55:6). The compassionate Hosea added his plea, "It is time to seek the Lord, till he come and rain righteousness upon you" (Hosea 10:12).

When the Apostle Paul stood in Athens to address the learned philosophers, he implored "that men would seek him [God] and perhaps reach out for him and find him, though he is not far from each one of us" (Acts 17:27, NIV).

Thus, when Jesus of Nazareth told his disciples that seeking and finding is an integral part of praying, he was in the mainstream of biblical teaching on spiritual discovery.

All of this emphasis on seeking and finding is to say that there are some prayer answers which we must find ourselves. This does not make it any less an activity of prayer. We should still take the need to God. We still trust God to answer, but we must allow him to answer as he chooses. And sometimes he chooses to answer by leading us to search and discover.

The first place to search for prayer answers is in the Bible itself. When the Word of God gives clear instructions, we already have our answer. We do not need to wait for further inspiration or instruction. We need only to act on the answer that is there. He will not give us a special message that contradicts his Word. We simply search the Scriptures, and do what he says there.

If we have not received the answer to a prayer we have been praying a good while, God may be wanting us to find the answer. The first place to start is in the Bible. The very answer we may have been waiting for may be waiting for us in the pages of God's Word.

In addition to answers which we can find in the Bible, there are answers all around us that God has waiting for our discovery. As Joseph Henry, the American physicist, said, "The seeds of great discoveries are constantly floating around us, but they only take root in minds well prepared to receive them."

A lot of times we interpret Jesus' words "seek and find" to mean that we should keep looking until we get what we want. What he means, instead, is that we should seek until we find what God has prepared for us. The found answer is the finding of God's will and God's provision.

In his autobiography *From Pagan to Christian,* Lin Yu-tang said:

> If I were God, and therefore a master chemist and physicist, I would be extremely interested in seeing how the chemists and astronomers and biologists on earth proceed to unlock my secrets. I would, of course, remain silent and give no help. But I would be very interested in watching their discoveries, giving them perhaps a century or two to pry open my secrets and think them over and work them out.

Jesus told a story about a man who was plowing a field and came across buried treasure. He said the kingdom of God is like that. Many treasures get added unexpectedly in the Christian pursuit of life.

One of our biggest surprises may be that we will discover our answers in our own backyard. In his famous lecture "Acres of Diamonds," Russell Conwell told the story of an ancient Persian named Al Hafed, who owned a large farm. One day a Buddhist priest told Al Hafed of the rich splendor of diamonds to be found in some parts of the world. Discontented, Al Hafed sold his farm and set out to search throughout the world for his fortune in diamonds. It was a fruitless search which left him discouraged and penniless, and he drowned himself in the sea. In the meantime, the person who had bought Al Hafed's farm discovered literally acres of diamonds on the land of the man who had plodded wearily over the earth seeking riches. We must not overlook the answers that may be the easiest to find and the closest to home.

In our meantime praying we have probably been asking God to do something. This is normal and it is the most common type of praying for all of us. I suggest that we ask God to open our eyes and help us find what he has already prepared for us.

Remember what Jeremiah told the exiles: "Ye shall seek me and find me when ye shall search for me with all your heart."

All of this implies an image of God that may be contrary to our usual picture of him when we pray. Perhaps we usually think of ourselves as waiting in faith and patience for the "God who acts." This is good and appropriate for received answers, but for the found answers of our lives, we need to get acquainted with the "God who waits."

Wallace Hamilton wrote that God "is not the Almighty Dictator, the Grand Sultan of the universe, pushing people around and snapping his fingers to get his will done in a hurry. He is the God who waits—with infinite patience he waits."

There is a double-edged sword in this word from Isaiah: "Therefore will the Lord wait, that he may be gracious unto you, and therefore will he be exalted, that he may have mercy upon you: for the Lord is a God of judgment: blessed are all they that wait for him" (Isaiah 30:18).

We are accustomed to being told that we should be like "those who wait for him," but Isaiah said in addition to our waiting for the Lord, that God is also waiting for us. Patiently, lovingly, God is waiting.

He waited a long time for men to grasp the idea of monotheism—faith in one God. He waited longer still for men to see their essential unity in brotherhood. He is still waiting for us to discover the way of peace.

God is not absent. He is simply patient. We have been thinking of ourselves as the patient ones, waiting on God to answer our prayers. Now, see God as the patient One, waiting on us to see and find the answers he has waiting for us.

Seeking and finding may be a risky business for us. It is so much more secure to stay where we are. But, there are things of God we cannot have until we are ready to leave the security of what God has done for the insecurity of what he is doing and will do.

In *The Explorer*, Rudyard Kipling sends a thrill through our hearts with the ringing challenge:

> Something hidden. Go and find it. Go and
>   look beyond the Ranges—
> Something long beyond the Ranges. Lost and
>   waiting for us. Go!

While we are waiting for things to work out, we may be able to use this interim for the most creative praying we have ever done. Deliberately and consciously, we should employ the seeking and finding concept of prayer and see how many answers we can make happen.

The secret to finding spiritual satisfaction is willingness to accept the given. When God gives, we must be willing to accept the gift. We cannot demand another gift which we may prefer. Our problem begins when we say, "That's not what I wanted, Lord," or "I think I'll keep working at it until I come up with something better."

A real prayer is not so much to gain an object as it is to fill a need. If I pray for medicine it is because my body is sick. If my body is well when the medicine arrives, I have no need for the medication for which I prayed; and yet, my real prayer—for restored health—has been abundantly answered.

We may be miserable in our jobs, but with a different attitude or different approach, we may change them into the dream situations. On the other hand, we may already know certain people who can open new doors.

We may know the kind of preparation necessary to advance or change; if so, we must act on it and find our answers.

We may be needing wisdom to make an important decision, but we keep closing our ears to what God is trying to tell us. Many times I have had people come to me for counseling, complaining that they have prayed and prayed but no answer has come. Often I have said, "But don't you see? When God leads you to someone for counseling, new ideas for action are suggested, and a new perspective is given, you are sitting in the very midst of God's unfolding answer."

We may be praying for a great place of service, wondering why God is not using us, and in our own neighborhood someone is lonely, destitute, and helpless. I heard a story about D. L. Moody, who was approached by a woman who told him that God had called her to preach. He said, "Thank God, dear lady, that he has so blessed you. Do you have a family?"

She replied, "Yes, I have a husband and ten children."

The great evangelist roared, "Then, Madam, you are twice blessed. Not only has God called you to preach, he has already given you a congregation. Now, go home and feed your flock."

We may be praying for skill and talent to serve God, but we are not exercising the talent we already have. I believe for every person we see with outstanding ability that there are a thousand more who are equipped to do the same if they just would. I am reminded so often of those poignant lines of Oliver Wendell Holmes:

> A few can touch the magic string,
> And noisy fame is proud to win them—
> Alas for those who never sing,
> But die with all their music in them.

We may be complaining that God hasn't spoken to us lately. We must be honest now. What did we do about the last thing he spoke to us about? I have learned that it is of little use asking God for some new message or some new gift if I haven't responded as he wanted me to when he last answered me. We ought not to expect God to give us something else until we have properly acted on his last revelation to us.

One of the saddest verses in the Bible is Jacob's comment upon awakening after the dream in which he saw God above the ladder. Jacob's words were, "Surely the Lord is in this place, and I was not aware of it" (Genesis 28:16, NIV). How tragic to miss God in all the places we journey! How wasteful to spend a life without being conscious of the divine presence! How drab never to see the miracles in the margin, and the answers to prayer all around us! Elizabeth Barrett Browning said it so beautifully:

> Earth's crammed with heaven
> And every common bush afire with God.
> But only he who sees takes off his shoes.
> All the rest sit around,
> And pick blackberries.

I know personally, from many long years of waiting, that it can look like God will never answer our prayers. But sooner or later the most patient divine preparation must land us on the threshold of fulfillment; the invisible spiritual process must come to the point. God prepares slowly to face us suddenly!

Our part is to be ready and to be willing to accept the answer when it comes. We must not forfeit the grand opportunity of being partners with God. We must not lose out on the joy of working in harmony with God, his world, and his plan for us. We must open the door and let the answer in.

8

Preparing for the Future

For thus saith the Lord, That after
seventy years be accomplished at
Babylon I will visit you, and perform
my good word toward you, in causing
you to return to this place. . . . And I
will be found of you, saith the Lord:
and I will turn away your captivity, and
I will gather you from all the nations,
and from all the places whither I have
driven you, saith the Lord; and I will
bring you again into the place whence
I caused you to be carried away
captive (Jeremiah 29:10, 14).

Every midnight is followed by dawn. Good Friday is followed by Easter. "Truth, crushed to earth, shall rise again" (William Cullen Bryant).

No meantime lasts forever. Our long waiting period will someday be over. Like every human experience, "This too shall pass away."

There are two grave errors that most of us make concerning the interim periods of our lives. First, we live as though they will never happen, ignoring our grandparents' old adage about "saving up for a rainy day."

The second mistake is living during the interim as though it will last forever. We lose our initiative, creativity, and optimism. We become pedantic, mundane, and pessimistic. The promises of our "false prophets" crash to earth. The rugs of hope are pulled out from under us again and again. We start accepting the unacceptable. Instead of living like human beings with vision and purpose, we live like animals concerned only with today's survival.

Then, one day relief comes, opportunity finally knocks, the door opens at last, dawn splashes across the horizon. And the tragedy is that so many of us are not ready. We are not prepared for the future. We do not expect the dawn. We are not equipped to handle our new opportunities.

Survival may be the first order of business for mean-time living, but it is not the last. While we are surviving the present, we must also be preparing for the future. If our prayers and faith are sincere, we believe that God is going to do something redemptive with our situation and provide us with a future. Are we preparing for that possibility?

When Abraham Lincoln's friends mocked him for studying so much during his youth, his steady reply was, "Some day my chance will come, and I want to be ready for it."

After the Babylonian exiles recovered from the shock of their defeat and began to adjust to life in a foreign land, they heeded Jeremiah's letter of instructions for living in the meantime. The most cherished part of the letter was the prophet's repeated promise that God would eventually bring them home again. He insisted that it would not be immediately, as their false prophets had said. In fact, he indicated it would be seventy years before the exiles and their descendants would see Jerusalem again.

By now the people had learned that Jeremiah was a true prophet. Everything else he had told them had been true, so they knew they could believe him about the return and restoration. Therefore, they decided that they should follow his advice about how to live in Babylon, but at the same time start getting things in order for the day of deliverance.

A young girl may fill her days with friends and activities while at the same time filling her "hope chest" for the coming years of marriage. A middle-aged couple can enjoy their families, friends, and occupations to the fullest while deliberately planning and saving for retirement. The wisest use of meantime days is to spend a part of them preparing for the future. This is what Israel did in Babylon.

The religious system that the world knows as Judaism today came out of the crises and changes precipitated by the Babylonian Exile. The father of modern day Judaism was not Abraham or Moses; he was Ezra, the scribe of the exile who went back to Jerusalem with Nehemiah to start the restoration. Ezra worked with the materials that had evolved during the exile. While waiting for their deliverance the Israelites shaped a whole new destiny for themselves.

Their estrangement from their homeland caused the Jews to draw closer to each other, developing a community bond, which exists to this day. They maintained communal organizations that followed patterns Samuel had set centuries before. "Elders" rose to places of increased influence and Ezekiel was the chief presider over the elders.

By their demeanor of forbearance and pride, the Jews won the respect of their captors and the vanquished regained their dignity. Jehoiachin, the king of Judah deported in 597 B.C., was brought out of prison by his Babylonian captors and given status among them. He dined at the king's table and was given an allowance for his personal needs (Jeremiah 52:31-34). Such honorable treatment enabled the Jews to maintain their feelings of national and religious identity.

The Jews began to adapt to Babylonian culture in

ways that benefitted them. For instance, they easily adopted the Aramaic language, which helped them in cultural and commercial exchanges. After the return from exile, Aramaic gradually replaced Hebrew as the language of Palestine. Thus, Aramaic was the language of Jesus and the apostles in New Testament times.

The exile also brought opportunity for dramatic vocational changes. Previously, the Israelites had traditionally been agricultural and pastoral people. In Palestine they had lived in "a land of grain and wine, a land of bread and vineyards, a land of olive trees and honey" (2 Kings 18:32). In Babylon these rural occupations were replaced by mercantile pursuits. Opportunities unknown to them in Palestine were now accessible in the "city of merchants." Many Jews became involved in Babylonian trade and business and began to accumulate experience and wealth. The fact that Jews are still renowned for their business acumen and ability to develop wealth began in the bitter experience of the exile.

There were other exiles, however, who were devoted to preserving the traditional faith. They saw their long estrangement as the consequence of sins and transgressions and sought to revitalize their worship of God. Some rituals, such as the practice of sacrifice, had to be discontinued in Babylon. But they could still pray with faces toward Jerusalem. Sabbath observance and circumcision were continued and given even more emphasis. The appearance of the synagogue also originated during the exile, giving the people a temporary "tabernacle" in a foreign land.

The exile also produced a dramatic alteration of Jewish theology and national destiny. The fall of Jerusalem had created a theological crisis for Israel. With Jerusalem destroyed and the temple gone, was Jehovah God also gone? The Jews were compelled to reexamine their traditional faith in God's protection of Israel. The old narrow provincialism gave way to a broader interpretation of God's concern, which now included other nations. Israel's destiny became more universal as she began to see herself now as "a light to the nations."

One of the most important results to emerge from the exile was the collecting and editing of the literature of Israel's faith. The world is indebted to the exile for giving Israel the time and incentive to assimilate and organize the great body of literature we know as the Old Testament.

The Torah rose to a new prominence because of the passing of traditional centers of Jewish loyalty. The cult of the north with the shrines of Dan and Bethel had been destroyed long ago. The covenant community of the old tribal league had no hope of being restored. Jews were scattered throughout the world, a situation known as the "Diaspora" (dispersion). The old bond of nationalistic cult no longer had meaning. The holy city of Jerusalem, revered as the sanctuary of God, was destroyed. The temple had been leveled to the ground and the Ark of the Covenant had disappeared. The Davidic dynasty appeared to be over, and all attempts to recapture the past were tragically disappointing.

What did Israel have left as a basis for community life on which to establish her continued existence? The key to survival was found in the Torah, the holy scriptures of Israel. They no longer had a holy city or a holy temple or a holy monarchy, but they still had the holy scriptures. They began to rally around the revealed word of God, and became obsessed with organizing it and preserving it. This emphasis led to Israel becoming known as a "people of the book."

During and after the exile the Torah was considered God's medium of revelation. When prophecy declined during the postexilic period, the Jews turned to the Torah to find God's final word to man. Eventually the law, the sacred Torah, came to be viewed as unchanging, unalterable, and eternal. By the time of the Christian era, the sacred writings were being extolled as the one possession left to Judaism apart from God himself. Although they had lost nearly everything else, the Jews had not lost their God, and they had not lost the holy scriptures he had given them. They had determined during the exile to prepare for the restoration of Israel by preserving the center of its faith.

I think we should now take these examples of the exiles and learn from them how we can prepare for our future so we will be ready for whatever opportunity comes when our meantime is over. There are seven basic actions which are suggested by the brief review we have just made of Israel in Babylon.

1. *Strengthen close relationships.* The communal life of Israel became stronger than it had ever been and welded them into an indestructible force.

Our church, our family, and our close friends should be a greater part of our lives now than ever. This is hard to do because the natural tendency is to withdraw from society when we are hurt or feel ashamed. Yet, that is the worst thing to do. This is the very time for us to run to church and family rather than running away.

2. *Maintain identity and dignity.* The Jews kept their national image intact and even their king was officially recognized as royalty in exile.

No one can take away our dignity but we ourselves. We must not allow adverse circumstances to drag us down and make us behave in a manner unbecoming to God, our family, and ourselves. People will continue to recognize us as the persons we recognize ourselves to be. If we want to come out of this trial with the same status and respect as when it began, then we must conduct ourselves exactly as "those" persons would.

3. *Adapt to constructive changes.* As indicated above, some changes are destructive and should be avoided, but others can help us if we are willing to be flexible. The Jews have always been proud of their Hebrew language, but it soon became obvious that survival in Babylon depended on their learning Aramaic. It wasn't too far removed from their native language and they stayed with it for centuries to follow.

We may have to learn a new language, change jobs, move to another neighborhood, make new friends, accept help from strangers, or get more education. But if we are willing to try something new, we may discover the key to unlock our prisons.

4. *Learn new skills or vocations.* Early Hebrew literature reflects Israel's love for the land and especially the pastoral vocations, but the Israelites were also a practical, pragmatic people. They knew how to change when it became necessary. So, the shepherds and farmers became merchants and bankers in the great metropolis of Babylon.

We may dearly love our old profession and cannot bring ourselves to think of doing something else, but our very future may depend on change. We may need to learn new skills or discover ways to use our old skills in a new job.

A friend of mine had been a missionary, a pastor, and finally a college president. Shortly after he began his academic career, I asked what was the most obvious thing he had learned in the transition. He said he had been strongly impressed by the fact that "skills are portable." There are many trades that can utilize diligence, manual dexterity, mechanical ability, and technological knowledge.

Likewise, there are numerous professions which require personality, leadership, sensitivity, and all the people-related skills. We must not box ourselves in by refusing to look at other options. We probably would do a lot better in a new job than we may imagine.

Hartman Hall was a survior of many meantimes because he knew the art of changing and learning new skills. Raising a family during lean years, he worked forty hours a week and attended night school until he became a C.P.A. Eventually he passed the state bar exam and became an attorney and counselor at law. When he became critically ill and was told that his blocked arteries were inoperable, he shifted his energies to the mission field of Togo, Africa, where his daughter and family were serving as missionaries. For ten years he lived in the "meantime" of waiting for the fatal blow to his heart, but during that meantime he had three trips to Togo, two of them to greet year-old granddaughters for the first time. He studied French in order to be able to communicate on his trips to Togo. At age sixty-four he learned the Morse Code and became a ham radio operator, talking frequently to ham operators in Africa and around the world. He used every interim situation as an opportunity to learn and grow.

5. *Reinforce essential beliefs.* The Jews intensified their religious traditions such as the Sabbath and circumcision. They instituted the synagogue when they had no temple.

If our beliefs are genuine and truly ours rather than tired hand-me-downs, we will discover their validity and strength during a meantime crisis.

Rufus Jones stressed the need for essential faith during interim stresses.

> Control over the peril of unsettlement is one of the main miracles of a genuinely religious way of life. Religious faith, when it comes to its true power, does just that miraculous thing for us all. It turns water to wine. It brings prodigals home. It sets men on their feet. It raises life out of death. It turns sunsets to sunrises. It makes the impossible become possible. The master secret of life is the attainment of the power of serenity in the midst of stress and action and adventure.

6. *Reconsider our position with God and others.* Before the exile the Jews had been extremely provincial, seeing themselves as the exclusive objects of God's loving concern. During the exile they began to develop a more universal spirit toward other nations and a more humble spirit toward themselves. During the exile, Babylon was overthrown by Persia, and Israel saw the Persians as the instruments of Jehovah God. Ezra began his account of the return and restoration like this: "This is what Cyrus king of Persia says: 'The Lord, the God of heaven, has given me all the kingdoms of the earth and he has appointed me to build a temple for him at Jerusalem in Judah'" (Ezra 1:2, NIV). Such a view of heathen kings would have been unthinkable before the exile.

As infants, we feel that our world is all the world, but as we mature we realize that the Father has other children whom he also loves. Realizing this should not diminish our feelings of self-worth or importance. It simply helps us get things in better perspective. It will also lift our spirits to realize that God has resources with which to work (even Cyrus, the Persian) that we may not even know.

Pain, either physical or emotional, intensifies self-consciousness and can almost blot out the reality of other people with their needs, their hurts, or even their comfort and strength. In my book, *And Stumbled on a Morning,* I wrote about the long nightmare when I was told I had MS:

> Because my hurt is uniquely mine, it's really hard for me to believe that others are suffering as much as I. Yet I know that self-pity is counterproductive in a healthy person, and it is absolutely destructive in the physically ill. Protection from this subtle enemy comes chiefly from the simple recognition that you are not the first nor the last to pass through this valley, and that your pain, as much as you hate to admit it, is probably not the worst.[1]

7. *Develop a lasting center of faith.* The Jews had gone through several centers of faith: the tabernacle, the Ark of the Covenant, the tribal league, nationalism, the temple, the holy monarchy, the city of Jerusalem. When all of those were gone they were left with their sacred writings, and they remain to this day a "people of the book."

The experiences we have had may have shattered many of our religious "centers." Now, we must back off and survey the wreckage. What do we have left? What can we afford to lose and still be a person of faith? Have we been trusting in perishable institutions, physical symbols, or imperfect human beings? Can we be disappointed in these or robbed of these and still believe in God? Are the Scriptures enough for us or must we have our own miracle or vision? Is Jesus the center of our faith (as the Torah became the center of Judaism), or have we placed a doctrine, a denomination, or a tradition at the center? Could we face the uncertain future if we were divested of our favorite theory, deserted by our best friends, disappointed by our strongest hero, and deprived of lifelong aids and symbols of religious faith?

The best preparation we can make for the future is to determine here and now what we can live without and still be a faithful, believing follower of Christ. The other side of that coin is to determine what we cannot and must not leave out of our lives. It simply means a recovery of center. Who or what is the basic center of our life and faith?

The disciples of Jesus turned a giant corner toward the future of Christianity when they faced this issue of center on the mount of transfiguration. When Peter wanted to build a tabernacle for Moses, Elijah, and Jesus, God emphasized the centrality of Jesus: "This is my beloved Son in whom I am well pleased; hear ye him." The disciples fell on their faces in fear and "when they had lifted their eyes, they saw no man, except Jesus only" (Matthew 17:1-8). Is "Jesus only" enough for us as we prepare for the future?

In preparing for the future, it is critically important that we do not give up until God has brought us through. In his message to which we have repeatedly referred, Dr. Marney said,

> People are always leaving the theater before the show is over. They never see the end of the play; nor hear the benediction. Sometimes even the actors throw up their hands and leave before the curtain falls. Thus did Judas—and thus do men today. Jeremiah is saying that there is a difference between the end of things

and the edge of things. He will say it again and again. There is a future from anywhere a person stands. He must quit marking off his own potential. He must not despair of anybody or anything until God gets through. As Chicken Little ran from an acorn, so man runs from life's normal meantimes as if an acorn, or any meantime could be an end of anything. There is a future from wherever he is, even when he can see the lights of the city.[2]

Realizing that there is indeed a future is the most vital necessity for living in the meantime. Viktor Frankl told of the problems he had in working with would-be suicides in the concentration camp. He said that each man who tried to take his own life believed that he had nothing more to expect from life. To counteract their despair, Frankl led them to realize that life was expecting something from them, that something in the future was expected of them. Frankl wrote:

A man who becomes conscious of the responsibility he bears toward a human being who affectionately waits for him, or to an unfinished work, will never be able to throw away his life. He knows the *why* for his existence, and will be able to bear almost any *how.*[3]

It is very possible that some of us may be thinking, "I have nothing to expect from life anymore." What we need is a fundamental change in attitude toward life. The important issue is not what we expect from life, but rather what life expects from us. Life ultimately means accepting the responsibility to find the right answers and to fulfill the tasks that are set before each of us. And this must be done even when it seems everything has been put on "hold."

Frankl called life in the concentration camp a "provisional existence," which seems to be an appropriate definition for any meantime situation. The unemployed worker, for example, is in a similar position. His existence has become provisional, and it is difficult for him to live for the future or aim at a goal. The Latin word *finis* has two meanings: the end or the finish, and a goal to reach. A man who cannot see the end of his "provisional existence" is not able to aim at an ultimate goal in life.[4]

It is a peculiarity of man that he can only live by looking to the future, and this is his salvation in the most difficult moments of his existence.

Our secretary's husband, John McClintic, was warden for several years at Texas' state penitentiary. In my many talks with him about the prisoners' state of mind during their "provisional existence," he constantly emphasized hope for the future as the number one essential for survival. He noted that even those who were serving life sentences believed that somehow they were going to be free some day.

I asked John if prisoners usually became depressed or hostile when they were turned down for parole. I was surprised when he told me that most of them just worked harder to make it next time, that the rejection of parole seemed to make them determined to try to control their destiny in the future. And usually these were the ones who eventually gained their freedom.

Even in our most hopeless meantime problem, we must not discount the trite words, "Don't lose hope." Experience repeatedly proves that those who keep believing and keep preparing for the future are the ones who some day step onto the threshold of a new day.

In order to help us prepare better for the future, we have marched through the seventy-year exile of the Jews in Babylon. This historical setting is a good model because it contains the major elements for survival and victory over a seemingly hopeless meantime. If they could do it, as dismal as their situation was, so can we.

Right now, we need to retrace the steps we have taken. We must be as open and as honest with ourselves as we possibly can. We must not dodge any question or minimize any issue we have raised. We cannot go around uncomfortable territory to get home; we must confront it and conquer it.

Recalling our first chapter, have we truly accepted the reality of things? Do we identify with the stages of grief outlined by Dr. Kübler-Ross? Do we fully understand the meaning and accept the responsibility implied by Viktor Frankl's insistence that the most important reality is the reality of choice and self-determination?

In our second chapter we were asked to see God behind the scenes. A posture or definition of faith was suggested for unbearable meantimes. Can we express verbally or write out our own understanding of the part faith plays in such times? Do we visualize God as *deus ex machina,* as Stockade, or as Center?

Getting back to work is the theme of the third chapter. Since reading it, have we determined on some concrete activity to get us back in the stream of things?

In chapter 4 the emphasis was on the family and the nurture of meaningful relationships. I have found that it is usually hardest to make amends with those who are the closest, but it is also the most rewarding. Have we taken at least the first step toward those who mean the most to us?

Burying the hatchet, advocated in chapter 5, requires humility and magnanimity. As Israel was urged to "pray for the peace of Babylon," have we started praying for the welfare of our enemies?

Chapter 6 contends that mature faith is able to recognize false prophets and reject false hope. Are we still listening to those who offer pious words and hollow hope, or have we learned to appreciate sincerity more?

As we were asked to consider prayer and seeking in chapter 7, did we understand the difference between prayer that receives and prayer that achieves? Are we willing to pray in the spirit of Christ as we seek God's help?

This brings us back to the last chapter and preparation for the future. In this chapter there are several suggestions for following Israel's examples in preparation. We need to go back over them and check the ones we have already done. How far are we from being ready for the next great thing God has waiting for us?

Viktor Frankl's survival from the concentration camp and eventual rise to become one of the world's most renowned psychologists is an inspiring example of the value of preparing for the future while enduring the worst of meantimes.

His words describing his release from the concentration camp are a fitting close to our sojourn through the meantime:

> One day, a few days after the liberation, I walked
> through the country past flowering meadows, for
> miles and miles, toward the market town near the
> camp. Larks rose to the sky and I could hear their
> joyous song. There was no one to be seen for miles
> around; there was nothing but the wide earth and sky
> and the larks' jubilation and the freedom of space. I
> stopped, looked around, and up to the sky—and then
> I went down on my knees. At that moment there was
> very little I knew of myself or of the world—I had but
> one sentence in mind—always the same: "I called to

the Lord from my narrow prison and He answered me in the freedom of space."

How long I knelt there and repeated this sentence memory can no longer recall. But I know that on that day, in that hour, my new life started. Step for step I progressed, until I again became a human being.[5]

NOTES AND SOURCES

Introduction
1. Carlyle Marney, "In the Meantime," in *Pastoral Preaching* (St. Louis: The Bethany Press, 1963), pp. 65, 66.
2. Ibid., p. 72.

Chapter 1
1. Bill Austin, *How to Get What You Pray For* (Wheaton, Ill.: Tyndale House Publishers, 1984), p. 112.
2. Marney, *Pastoral Preaching*, p. 67.
3. Elisabeth Kübler-Ross, *On Death and Dying* (New York: Macmillan Publishing Co., Inc., 1969), pp. 38, 39.
4. Ibid., p. 39.
5. Carl Rogers, *On Becoming a Person* (Boston: Houghton Mifflin, 1961).
6. Andras Angyal, *Foundations for a Science of Personality* (London: Oxford University Press, 1941), p. 94.
7. Rufus Jones, *Rufus Jones Speaks to Our Time,* edited by Harry Emerson Fosdick (New York: Macmillan Publishing Co., Inc., 1958), p. 226.
8. Viktor E. Frankl, *Man's Search for Meaning* (New York: Simon and Schuster, 1939, 1963), p. 21.
9. Ibid., p. 22.
10. Ibid., p. 115.
11. Ibid., p. 131.
12. Ibid., p. 30.
13. Ibid., p. 206.
14. Ibid., pp. 103, 104.

Chapter 2
1. Austin, *How to Get What You Pray For,* pp. 96, 97.
2. Paul Scherer, *The Word God Sent* (New York: Harper and Row Publishers, 1965), p. 227.

3. David O. Woodyard, *The Opaqueness of God* (Philadelphia: Westminster Press, 1970), p. 47.
4. Charles Hartshorne, *Man's Vision of God* (Chicago: Willett, Clark and Company, 1941), p. 293.
5. Helmut Thielicke, *The Waiting Father* (New York: Harper and Row Publishers, 1959), p. 29.
6. J. B. Phillips, *Your God Is Too Small* (New York: Macmillan Publishing Co., Inc., 1961), pp. 15-59.
7. Vernard Eller, *His End Up* (Nashville: Abingdon Press, 1969), pp. 26, 27.
8. Ibid., p. 31.
9. Ibid., p. 34.
10. C. W. Christian, *Shaping Your Faith* (Waco: Word Books, 1973), p. 179.
11. Helmut Thielicke, *How to Believe Again* (Philadelphia: Fortress Press, 1970), p. 192.

Chapter 3
1. Marney, *Pastoral Preaching*, p. 68.
2. Jones, *Rufus Jones Speaks*, p. 227.

Chapter 4
1. Marney, *Pastoral Preaching*, pp. 68, 69.
2. Frankl, *Man's Search*, p. vii.
3. Ibid., pp. 58, 59.
4. Trueblood, *Recovery*, pp. 49-53.

Chapter 5
1. Frankl, *Man's Search*, p. 137.
2. Marney, *Pastoral Preaching*, pp. 69-71.

Chapter 6
1. Frankl, *Man's Search*, p. 53.
2. Ibid., p. 132.

Chapter 7
1. Most of the material in this chapter has been developed from my book *How to Get What You Pray For*, pp. 153-161.

Chapter 8
1. Bill Austin, *And Stumbled on a Morning* (Wheaton, Ill.: Tyndale House Publishers, 1979), pp. 31-32.
2. Marney, *Pastoral Preaching,* pp. 69-71.
3. Frankl, *Man's Search,* p. 127.
4. Ibid., p. 112.
5. Ibid., p. 141.